Map Legend

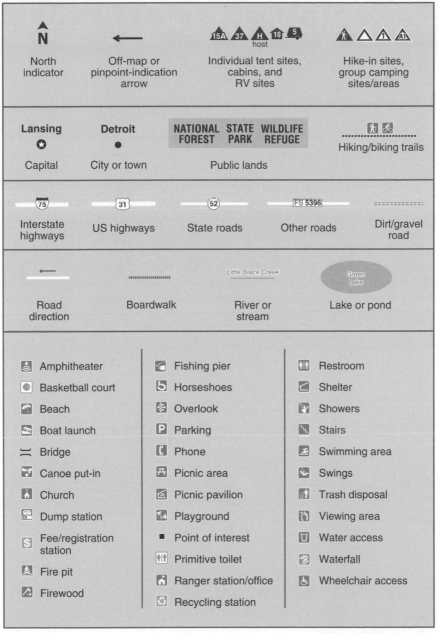

N ↑	←	15A 37 H host 10 5	🚶 △ △ △
North indicator	Off-map or pinpoint-indication arrow	Individual tent sites, cabins, and RV sites	Hike-in sites, group camping sites/areas

Lansing ✪	**Detroit** ●	NATIONAL FOREST STATE PARK WILDLIFE REFUGE	🚶 🚴 Hiking/biking trails
Capital	City or town	Public lands	

75	31	52	FS 5396	
Interstate highways	US highways	State roads	Other roads	Dirt/gravel road

←		*Little Black Creek*	*Green Lake*
Road direction	Boardwalk	River or stream	Lake or pond

🎭 Amphitheater	🎣 Fishing pier	🚻 Restroom
⚫ Basketball court	🔩 Horseshoes	◤ Shelter
🏖 Beach	🏞 Overlook	🚿 Showers
🚣 Boat launch	P Parking	🪜 Stairs
⤫ Bridge	📞 Phone	🏊 Swimming area
🛶 Canoe put-in	🏕 Picnic area	🤸 Swings
⛪ Church	🏠 Picnic pavilion	🗑 Trash disposal
🚽 Dump station	🛝 Playground	🔭 Viewing area
S Fee/registration station	■ Point of interest	🚰 Water access
🔥 Fire pit	🚻 Primitive toilet	💦 Waterfall
🪵 Firewood	🏠 Ranger station/office	♿ Wheelchair access
	♻ Recycling station	

ACKNOWLEDGMENTS

Many people contributed to this book with helpful information and by sharing some of their favorite places to camp. I first want to thank the hardworking people at the Michigan Department of Natural Resources and the U.S. Forest Service. They do a bang-up job of providing the best campgrounds around.

Michigan has well over a thousand campgrounds—more than any one person can fully appreciate. Numerous camping friends made sure their favorites weren't lost in the shuffle; they all shared their experiences of camping in Michigan and gave me productive suggestions. Likewise, the folks who take time to post and respond on my *Best Tent Camping: Michigan* Facebook page (facebook.com/michigantentcamping) are always quick with suggestions and top-notch advice for campers.

Finally, I would like to thank you, the people who regularly leave home and live for a while in tents. By doing so, you support the state's campgrounds. Without a community of active and conscientious campers, outdoor recreation in Michigan wouldn't be the same. Keep camping, and I hope to see you out there!

—Matt Forster

PREFACE

I love camping in Michigan. Every campground here sits alongside some body of water—be it a river, stream, pond, or lake. (Perhaps it's the negative ions these waters generate that leave you feeling peaceful and relaxed after a week out in nature.) From grassy dunes overlooking Lake Michigan to thick woods along the Pine River to a quiet lake that serves as a portal to the Sylvania Wilderness, pitching a tent in Michigan opens the door to all sorts of adventure.

The largest state east of the Mississippi, Michigan is a land made for camping. Nowhere in the state are you ever farther than 85 miles from a Great Lake. With 36,000 miles of rivers and streams and 11,000 inland lakes, the state is a camper's paradise, whether you've come to fish, paddle, swim, or hike. Thousands of miles of trails await backpackers and mountain bikers—plus you have the North Country Trail winding its way along the length of both peninsulas.

Water tends to be the real attraction here, and it is water that has largely determined Michigan's history. When major transportation routes were synonymous with rivers and lakes, the Great Lakes constituted a great highway. European explorers found they could penetrate deeper into the continent without the grueling job of hauling supplies and gear through untamed forest and over unfamiliar mountains if they simply loaded a canoe and followed the water. Of course, hauling a boat and luggage over rapids and across miles of portage was no easy task, but it beat the alternatives.

With the advent of the locomotive and then the automobile, land routes began to dominate, and the great bodies of water that would continue to play an important role in transporting Michigan lumber, copper, and iron became an obstacle to the general east-to-west flow of the nation. If you look at a map today, none of the east–west interstate highways even cross into Michigan. (Aside from I-75, which begins at the southern end of Florida and ends in Sault Ste. Marie, you won't find any interstates at all north of the southernmost third of Michigan's Lower Peninsula.) Of course, cities don't base their value on their proximity to a freeway, but these transportation hubs can tell you a lot about where businesses and people are in the state.

All of this is an incredible gift to people who like to go camping in tents. Most of the state's industry is found in a small swath of southern counties, and this leaves the rest of the state open to recreation. And while you'll find excellent places to camp in the southern Lower Peninsula, it's the northern part of the "mitten" and the Upper Peninsula where you'll find sprawling state and national forests with hundreds of excellent campgrounds.

People have their own reasons for getting out into nature: exercise, relaxation, the pride of self-sufficiency. Lately, people have begun to enjoy "technology fasts"—simply leaving the world of phones, email, and social media behind to reset the mind, to reestablish a natural rhythm to their thinking. Whatever your reasons, I hope you find this guide a helpful resource. Be sure to let me know what you think, and keep camping!

—M. F.

BEST CAMPGROUNDS

BEST FOR FUN WITH FAMILIES

BEST FOR SCENIC BEAUTY

BEST FOR FISHING

BEST FOR HIKING

Beachgoers explore Warren Dunes in southwest Michigan (see Campground 12, page 47).

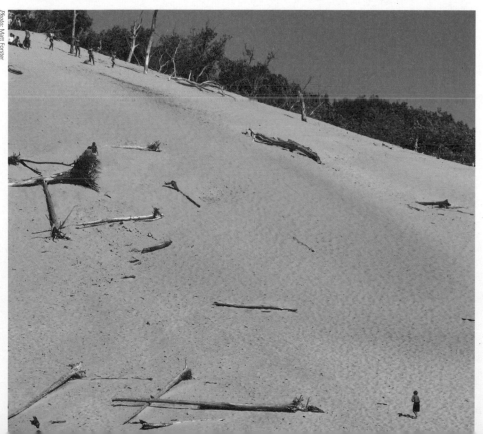

BEST FOR HIKING *(continued)*

BEST FOR CYCLING AND MOUNTAIN BIKING

BEST FOR CANOEING AND KAYAKING

BEST FOR SWIMMING

BEST FOR PEACE AND QUIET

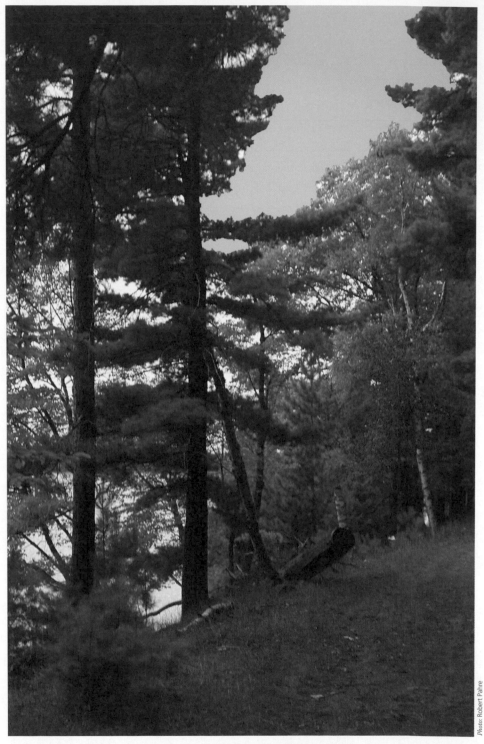

Autumn's first red leaves along Clark Lake (see Campground 49, page 163)

Photo: Robert Pahre

INTRODUCTION

A WORD ABOUT THIS BOOK AND MICHIGAN TENT CAMPING

As I travel throughout Michigan, I always like to check out the local real estate listings—especially the magazines that feature vacation property. Even as home prices have fallen around the country, small vacation homes still list for hundreds of thousands of dollars—millions for homes on waterfront property. A 100-foot-wide lot on Lake Michigan can start at half a million dollars just for the acreage.

Thousands of people carry a humbler dream of a cottage in the woods on one of Michigan's smaller inland lakes. And even those who can scrimp and save for a summer getaway are often disappointed when the lot next door is bought by a well-to-do family from the city who erects a gaudy McMansion 5 feet off the property line. It's a common story to hear of once-remote hideaways that now look like the very subdivisions their owners were trying to escape in the first place.

Thankfully, there is another way to enjoy the natural beauty of Michigan. In my mind, the best places to spend your free time are those graciously provided by the state park system and the National Park Service, as well as by numerous counties and townships: Michigan's campgrounds. The choicest pieces of land around the state of Michigan have been set aside for the enjoyment of anyone with a tent and a few bucks. Million-dollar views can be had for less than the price of a cheap hotel—often for much less. Those willing to tackle a little adventure will enjoy remote beaches, waterfalls, and scenic woodland hikes far from the madding crowd.

The nearly 20 state parks along Lake Michigan, for example, boast miles of sandy beach (much of it rarely seen by more than a few visitors), wooded campsites, rivers and lakes for fishing, and an extensive collection of trails for hiking and biking. And at Sleeping Bear National Lakeshore, campers can enjoy a secluded campsite, take a long walk on the beach, explore the dunes, and tour quaint towns and villages along US 31—maybe even make the scenic drive to Traverse City, northern Michigan's premier vacation city.

Michigan's Upper Peninsula, on the other hand, has some of the best wilderness camping in the Midwest at Isle Royale National Park and the Porcupine Mountains Wilderness State Park. The North Country Trail, which crosses seven states on its way from New York to North Dakota, follows the shore of Lake Superior, connecting the Porkies in the west with the Pictured Rocks National Lakeshore farther east. In the southwest Upper Peninsula, the Sylvania Wilderness Area has backcountry camping for those who carry their gear in a canoe rather than a backpack or car trunk.

Even close to metro Detroit, state parks and southeast Michigan's Metroparks have stellar camping facilities close to town but worlds away from the strip malls and shopping centers of civilization.

I've camped all over Michigan, and in this guide I bring to you what I believe are the 50 finest locations in the state for tent camping. Tent campers have a unique perspective when it comes to spending their free time. More important to these folks than electricity, cable TV, a game room, and level cement slabs is a picturesque wooded site that offers enough quiet and solitude to enjoy nature and the company of friends and family.

My intention in writing this guide is to provide the information you need to make your next Michigan camping trip the best yet. I hope you enjoy these campgrounds as much as I have.

HARD CHOICES: ISLE ROYALE NATIONAL PARK

Trying to whittle the list of 1,200 or so campgrounds in Michigan down to 50 is a daunting task. You may skim the sites here and find that your favorite didn't make the cut. I'll be straight: a *lot* of great campgrounds didn't make the cut. Paddlers, anglers, mountain bikers, and hikers all have different requirements and preferences when it comes to camping. For aesthetic reasons, some folks enjoy a wide-open, grassy site overlooking a lake; others prefer a dark niche carved out of thick woods, set apart from the nearby river. I hope there's something in here for everyone.

That said, one notable omission here merits special mention. More than 40 miles north of the Keweenaw Peninsula in Lake Superior, Isle Royale National Park is composed of a long 207-square-mile island and the nearly 400 smaller islands that surround it.

To say that opportunities for camping at Isle Royale are numerous would be an understatement. (As this is a book about camping, it seemed a shame to have to pick just one from the bunch and reduce the entire park to just that description.) Backpacking routes traverse the island from end to end. Ferries can get you to several campgrounds near the shore, though most visitors come to hike. Many people bring canoes and crisscross along the island's inland lake. Still others use sea kayaks to explore the island from the waters of Lake Superior. However you choose to enjoy the park, you share the wilderness with its full-time residents, including a thriving population of wolves and moose.

You will also find evidence of human history here—surprising in a place so remote. American Indians were mining copper on the island as early as the fourth century BC. These ancient mining sites are still visible, as are other pieces of the island's history, including lighthouses and shipwrecks.

Getting to Isle Royale is always the big question. Campers ferry to the island from Houghton, Michigan (a 6.5-hour trip); Copper Harbor, Michigan (a 4.5-hour trip); and Grand Portage, Minnesota (a 2- to 3-hour trip, depending on the ferry). This adds significantly to any trip. For example, if you live in or around metro Detroit, the drive to Houghton is 9.5 hours. Once there, you find a room for the night and then wake the next morning to catch the ferry, another 6.5 hours to the first stop on the island. If your plans take you around to a campground on the island's far side, you could be looking at another day on the boat before you pitch your tent. That's two very full days before you even step onto Isle Royale.

The simple reason for omitting Isle Royale from this volume is that the park offers so much—and requires so much in the way of skills, knowledge, and experience—that it really deserves an entire book to itself, and any mention we might make would be inadequate in preparing a camper for the experience. Fortunately, there's just such a book that offers the information you need to plan a trip of this scale: *Isle Royale National Park: Foot Trails & Water Routes,* by Jim DuFresne, is the definitive guide to the island and has been used by thousands.

HOW TO USE THIS GUIDEBOOK

THE RATINGS AND RATINGS CATEGORIES

Evaluating campgrounds requires some finesse, and in the end it's more of an art than a science. For a quick summary of what qualities make these campgrounds worth visiting, each is rated on a five-star scale for six attributes: beauty, privacy, spaciousness, quiet, security, and cleanliness.

Not every campground in this book can pull a high score in every category. Sometimes a very worthwhile campground is located on terrain that makes it difficult to provide a lot of space, for example; in these cases, look for high marks in beauty or quiet to trump room to stretch out. In every case, the star-rating system is a handy tool to help you pinpoint the campground that will fit your personal requirements.

★★★★★ The site is **ideal** in that category.

★★★★ The site is **exemplary** in that category.

★★★ The site is **very good** in that category.

★★ The site is **above average** in that category.

★ The site is **acceptable** in that category.

BEAUTY

Some campsites are so perfectly placed—nestled in cedars and white paper birch or on a bluff overlooking dunes—that it's hard to leave camp. Others are located with easy access to long stretches of Great Lakes shoreline with warm beaches and stunning sunsets (or sunrises, as the case may be). This rating accounts for both the beauty of the site and that of the general area.

PRIVACY

No one likes to duck out of a tent first thing in the morning to see neighbors brushing their teeth and spitting into the bushes just feet away. The best campgrounds keep sight lines to a minimum and allow bushes and trees to act as natural barriers.

SPACIOUSNESS

Fire pits quickly become a gathering place when folks are out camping. Campsites should have enough room for people to enjoy the fire with space to park the car, pitch a tent, and set up a dining area away from the flames. And if there's room for a hammock or clothesline, all the better.

QUIET

Some parks tend to attract rowdy crowds from Memorial Day through Labor Day. Groups of children running through the campsites and grown-ups playing music long into the night are not everyone's idea of camping. Other campgrounds are relatively peaceful throughout the season. (Keep in mind, however, that any public campground can attract a party crowd, especially on holiday weekends. Thankfully, this situation isn't as likely at the more remote locations.)

SECURITY

Campground hosts, park rangers, and gates that are closed after-hours can make a campground much more secure. Other campgrounds are far from civilization, and their remoteness can be both a source of security and a liability. In general, Michigan campgrounds are very safe, secure, and family-friendly.

CLEANLINESS

Each campground is rated on its overall cleanliness. Bathrooms and showers, camp stores, and other common areas are inspected and rated. It's also important that the sites themselves are clear of litter and the reminders of previous campers.

THE CAMPGROUND PROFILE

Here's where you'll find the nitty-gritty details. Not only is the property described, but readers can also get a general idea of the recreational opportunities available—what's in the area and perhaps suggestions for touristy activities.

THE CAMPGROUND LOCATOR MAP AND MAP LEGEND

To find the best campground in a specific part of the state, begin with the Michigan Campground Locator Map (page iv), which shows you where all 50 campgrounds are located. Each campground's number appears not only on the locator map but also in the table of contents on the facing page and on each campground profile's first page. A legend that details the symbols found on the campground-layout maps (see below) appears immediately following the table of contents, on page v.

CAMPGROUND-LAYOUT MAPS

Each campground profile includes a more detailed map showing campsites, roads, facilities, and other key elements. Note that in recent years budget cuts have required the state to reduce the size of some campgrounds (and to close others), so while these maps were accurate at the time of this writing, please be aware that conditions on the ground can change.

GPS CAMPGROUND-ENTRANCE COORDINATES

Backpackers and campers were among the first groups to adopt GPS technology. Now that seemingly everyone has a box on their dashboard that squawks directions, or an app on their phone that does the same, it makes sense to include this information here. (*Note:* A dedicated GPS unit will easily guide you to any of these campgrounds, but users of mobile GPS apps may find that cell service is unavailable in remote areas.)

We provide each campground's location in latitude–longitude format, expressed in degrees and decimal minutes. For example, the GPS coordinates for Holly Recreation Area: McGinnis Lake Campground (page 11) are as follows:

N42° 48.994' W83° 31.515'

To convert GPS coordinates from degrees, minutes, and seconds to the above degrees and decimal minutes, divide the seconds by 60. For more on GPS technology, visit usgs.gov.

WEATHER

Michigan weather is rather predictable. Rain is pretty common in the spring and fall. Throughout the summer, temperatures are warm and the air can be very humid; thunderstorms are common.

But although the weather faithfully follows the seasons, the seasons themselves are inconsistent throughout the state. Summer in the Upper Peninsula begins much later and ends much sooner. Fall colors that blaze in the Upper Peninsula in September take a month or more to reach the lower half of the Lower Peninsula. Even in the height of summer, the nights up north can be chilly. Closer to the lakes, weather changes more rapidly, but weather stations often have a good idea of what's coming ahead of time.

Tornadoes are a concern during their traditional season of spring and summer (but be aware that tornadoes have been reported year-round). In the event of a tornado, seek shelter. If you get caught out in the open, lie down in any sort of ditch you can find.

FLORA AND FAUNA PRECAUTIONS

Michigan's wildlife rarely causes campers much difficulty. Deer, of course, are always a road hazard toward dusk—on average, the state witnesses 40,000 car–deer crashes annually. Most occur in the southern half of the Lower Peninsula, but that's probably because there is more traffic in that region of the state.

TICKS aren't as much of a problem in Michigan as they are in other states. These arachnids are typically found on low-hanging branches waiting for unsuspecting passersby (they're hoping for deer). Tick-borne illness is not unheard of, and Lyme disease and Rocky Mountain spotted fever are just two of the illnesses that ticks can carry (the tiny deer tick, shown below, carries the former).

Deer tick

Photo: Jim Gathany/Centers for Disease Control and Prevention (public domain)

After a hike through wooded and heavily grassy areas, it's a good idea to have a partner take a look at your back to be sure none of these buggers have nestled in. If you do find one embedded in your skin, use fine-tipped tweezers to pinch the tick as near to the skin as possible, and slowly pull straight up. Thoroughly clean the bite and your hands with rubbing alcohol or soap and water. If you later feel ill or if a red, ringlike rash appears around the removal site, see a doctor.

BLACKFLIES In the Upper Peninsula especially, blackflies are prodigious enough to make even a hardcore camper downright ornery. From mid-May to July, their populations swell; with their painful bite, they can make outdoor activity north of the bridge unbearable. Repellents are not terribly effective, and most die-hard outdoor enthusiasts who brave the fly season recommend long-sleeved shirts and pants and even nets to protect your head and neck.

MOSQUITOES Though these insects can carry illnesses such as West Nile virus, in Michigan mosquitoes are more a nuisance than anything else. Repellents powered by DEET have proved the most effective; if you don't like the chemical on your skin, wear long sleeves and pants, and spray your clothing.

BLACK BEARS Most campers who get a look at one of Michigan's black bears are more excited at the opportunity than frightened. Fewer than 20,000 of these notoriously shy animals roam the northern woods—90% of those are in the Upper Peninsula. When camping in bear country, be sure to keep your camp clean. Properly dispose of garbage, and store food in a vehicle or a hanging bear bag.

Black bears typically avoid humans, but if you're approached by a bear, try to scare it off by yelling and making yourself look big—don't bolt and run or climb a tree. If the bear attacks, *fight back,* beating it off with any implement at hand. Playing dead is not an effective strategy.

POISON IVY More common than a black bear but harder to come by than a mosquito, poison ivy can make a trip very uncomfortable—and for those who are allergic, it can be deadly. The plant is recognizable by its three leaflets per leaf (inspiring the phrase "leaves of three, let it be"). Urushiol, the oil in the plant, causes a painful, itchy rash when it comes in contact with the skin.

Poison ivy

If you discover that you've crunched through a patch of poison ivy, vigorously wash your exposed skin as soon as possible; then apply calamine lotion and/or an anti-itch cream. (My grandma taught us to use Lava soap to remove the oil before a rash springs up, and that has always worked well for me in the past.) Likewise, make sure to wash any clothes, pets, or hiking gear that may have touched the plant—it's not unheard of to experience a second outbreak of a poison ivy rash a year after the first because you picked up a pair of shoes that were never properly cleaned.

FIRST AID KIT

A first aid kit is an essential piece of gear, especially if your camping trips involve hiking, mountain biking, or other recreational activities. Even collecting wood for the evening fire has its share of risks, however. Outfitters such as REI and Moosejaw sell prepackaged kits, as do stores such as Target and Walmart. Read the label and be sure the kit you purchase (or assemble) has the following:

- Ace bandages or Spenco joint wraps
- Adhesive bandages
- Antibiotic ointment (such as Neosporin)
- Antihistamine (such as Benadryl), for mild allergies
- Antiseptic or disinfectant (such as Betadine or hydrogen peroxide)
- Aspirin, acetaminophen (Tylenol), or ibuprofen (Advil)
- Butterfly-closure bandages

- Comb and tweezers (for removing ticks from your skin)

- Emergency/survival blanket

- Epinephrine (EpiPen), for serious allergies

- Gauze (one roll and six 4-by-4-inch compress pads)

- LED flashlight or headlamp

- Matches or lighter

- Mirror (for signaling rescuers)

- Moist towelettes

- Moleskin/Spenco 2nd Skin

- Pocketknife or multipurpose tool

- Waterproof first aid tape

- Whistle (if you get lost or hurt)

New campers should consider taking a first aid class or, at the very least, picking up one of the many quick guides to first aid that you can find at your favorite outfitter.

PLANNING THE PERFECT TRIP

The key to any successful camping trip is in the planning. As we Boy Scouts recited in mantralike fashion, "The prepared Scout is a happy Scout." For me, this has proved true more often than not. For car campers who keep a vehicle nearby, there is no good reason not to bring along those little extras—an extra pair of socks, an extra wool blanket, and such.

- **RESERVE YOUR CAMPSITE.** Camping is popular in Michigan, so much so that certain campgrounds will be completely booked even before the season is under way. Last-minute campers will almost always find a site somewhere, but those who want a *particular* somewhere will need to plan ahead. To reserve campsites at Michigan state parks and recreation areas, call 800-447-2757 or go to midnrreservations.com; sites located in federal lands can be reserved by phone at 877-444-6777 or online at recreation.gov. Both systems charge a one-time, refundable reservation fee; check the websites for specifics. Other campgrounds can be called in advance.

- **PREPARE FOR THE WEATHER.** It goes without saying that raingear is essential. Campers also need warm clothing, especially in the spring and fall. When consulting the weather forecast before a trip, be sure to note the nighttime lows. Many campers who come prepared only for 60° days will spend an awful night shivering when it drops into the 30s. Other essentials include a pack of playing cards and a book or two. If you have to be stuck in a tent all day, it's good to have something to do.

- **CONSIDER YOUR TENT SITE.** The best place to pitch your tent is on level ground. Avoid tree roots and rocks. Also try to imagine where water might flow if it rains. Often the smoothest ground is that which has been washed clean by regular runoff from a nearby hill. And to avoid mosquitoes infiltrating your temporary abode, try to keep some distance from bushes and tall grass.

- **CONSIDER YOUR CAMPING COLLEAGUES.** One of Ernest Hemingway's characters famously said, "Never go on trips with anyone you do not love." The question I would ask is, "How do you know you love someone until you've gone on a trip together?" A camping trip can be a great bonding experience, but you should realize that not everyone approaches the art of camping from the same perspective, and you need to make allowances when camping with new people.

   I once sat waiting for dinner while two friends of mine argued over the amount of time it takes to boil water before it's safe to drink. One said 3 minutes; the other said 10. (Interestingly, if you search online for this information, you'll find the same debate still raging among supposed experts.) After a few days, this kind of argument can ruin a trip. It's always best to remain gracious in the woods.

CAMPING ETIQUETTE

Here are a few more guidelines to consider as you prepare for your trip.

- **BE A GOOD NEIGHBOR.** The Golden Rule—"Treat your neighbor as you yourself would like to be treated"—applies to camping as much as it does to life in general. Watch your noise in camp. Don't leave your garbage about. And keep the kids from running willy-nilly through others' sites.

- **FOLLOW THE RULES.** You've heard that good fences make good neighbors? Campground rules are established to maintain a sense of order in a public place used by many different people. Not only do the rules help campground staff go about their business, they act as a fence between campers. In general, things like following the posted quiet hours and taking care of your trash help to maintain amiable relations between strangers.

- **RESPECT THE WILDERNESS.** When camping in wilderness areas, follow a strict carry-in/carry-out policy. It's frustrating when others leave a mess behind, thereby spoiling the experience for those who follow.

- **BUY THE PROPER PERMITS.** The **Michigan Recreation Passport** ($11 at the time of this writing) can be purchased by (1) Michigan residents when they register their automobile license plates and (2) nonresidents at state parks, recreation areas, Department of Natural Resources (DNR) customer service centers, and online at michigan.gov/recreationpassport. Though you may feel like you're getting nickel-and-dimed to death, these fees provide the necessary funds to pay park staff and maintain the campgrounds we love.

CANOE CAMPING

Michigan isn't Minnesota, where the canoe is practically ingrained into the camping culture, but the states do share many traits, and wilderness paddlers have plenty of waterways to keep them occupied. Rivers, lakes, ponds, and streams are everywhere. In Michigan, you're never more than 6 miles from an inland lake. As such, the region is especially suited for wilderness paddling. Even in southeast Michigan, within minutes of the 'burbs, state recreation areas have special campsites set aside for paddlers.

ROASTING MARSHMALLOWS

An important topic that often goes ignored in camping guides is a proper discussion of marshmallows. The name of this delicious treat comes from *Althaea officinalis,* or the common marshmallow, a flowering plant whose leaves, flowers, and roots were used for their medicinal properties. The ancient Egyptians were perhaps the first to see the confectionary value of the marshmallow, but it wasn't until the French added egg white and rose water to create *pâté de guimauve* that we saw a treat resembling the marshmallows we buy today. Interestingly enough, commercially available marshmallows these days are made primarily of sugar with some other ingredients to fluff them up (that is, "no marshmallows were harmed in the making of these marshmallows").

No one knows, of course, who came up with the idea of toasting marshmallows over an open fire. Whoever it was deserves a statue somewhere. Seriously. More than a tasty treat, roasted marshmallows have become a time-honored tradition here in the United States. When friends get together to sit around a campfire, it's time to gather some long sticks or roasting forks and open a bag of marshmallows. This warm, sugary treat is even better when stuffed between two graham crackers with a square of chocolate.

A certain etiquette applies when it comes to roasting marshmallows over a campfire. Most of the rules are just different ways of respecting individual preferences because people come at the task in different ways. Some are attracted to the flicker of the flame and delight as sugar is transformed into heat, what we call the flaming torch–mallow. Then there are the contemplative types, campers who carefully lay claim to the white-hot heat of the coals and slowly turn their sticks to create that perfect allover tan.

Whatever your inclination—whether you like your marshmallows hard in the middle with a crunchy black shell or lightly toasted yet warmed through and through (personally, I like a golden trunk topped with a slightly charred mushroom cap of burnt sugar)—as my daughter's Berenstain Bears video teaches, "People like different things, and that's OK."

For practical purposes, having enough sticks on hand is as important as remembering the Hershey's bars. When you only have one stick, the roaster is commonly expected to wait until everyone's had a bite before joining in. This can be a rough wait.

When there are enough roasting sticks for the whole gang, it's important to respect boundaries. That is, don't cross sticks. When someone is carefully rotating a marshmallow for the perfect golden color, reaching over his stick with your stick can prevent the timely removal of the marshmallow from the heat. Pretty soon, someone's not paying attention, sticks clash, and everyone's marshmallows end up in the ashes.

It's also wise, with so many people leaning over an open fire with hot melted sugar on the end of pointy sticks or metal roasting forks, to pay attention. Marshmallows on the ground can be a bummer, but it's all fun and games until someone gets a poker in the eye.

SOUTHEAST MICHIGAN

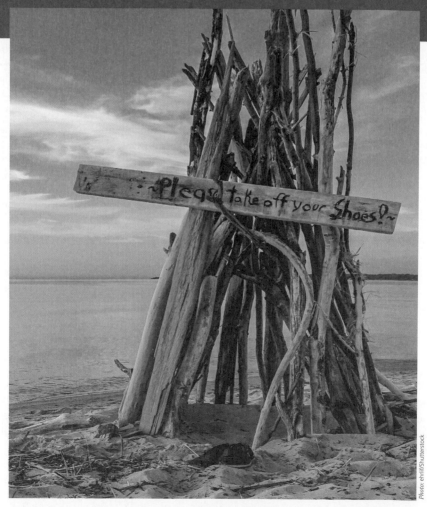

Heed the sign! A driftwood beach hut welcomes visitors to Port Crescent State Park (see Campground 4, page 21).

⛺ Holly Recreation Area:
MCGINNIS LAKE CAMPGROUND

Beauty ★★★★ Privacy ★★★ Spaciousness ★★★★ Quiet ★★★ Security ★★★★ Cleanliness ★★★★★

Just beyond the reach of the suburbs, Holly Rec offers many Michiganders the feel of Up North without the drive.

Located in northern Oakland County, Holly Recreation Area is nearly 8,000 acres of steep rolling hills and small woodland lakes, the indelible reminders of the glaciers that once covered our humble peninsula. To put that into perspective, the acreage at Holly Rec adds up to 12.5 square miles. The state has turned the area into a showcase park for outdoor recreation. There's something here for everyone—miles of trails for hiking and cross-country skiing, beaches for swimming, and lakes for paddling and fishing. The park also maintains one of the area's best disc golf courses. The course has 24 baskets, with routes that allow players to toss for 9, 18, or 24 holes.

Separate from the main park—west of the expressway on Grange Hall Road—Holly Rec also has trails set aside solely for mountain biking. These trails are serious business, with three loops (graded for ability) that add up to more than 23 miles of off-road pedaling.

The main day-use area and the campground are separated by McGinnis Road. If you're looking for a campground that's just a short walk away from the swimming beach, this isn't

Tamarack swamps surround McGinnis Lake Campground.

Photo: Michelle Caldwell (public domain)

KEY INFORMATION

CONTACT: Michigan DNR–Holly State Recreation Area, 248-634-8811, michigan.gov/holly; reservations: 800-447-2757, midnrreservations.com

OPEN: Aspen Loop, late April–November; late March–November for other loops

SITES: 15 semimodern, 144 modern

EACH SITE HAS: Picnic table and fire pit

ASSIGNMENT: Online or by phone

REGISTRATION: At park office

AMENITIES: Electricity, water, hot showers, modern restrooms, and pit toilets

PARKING: At sites

NIGHTLY FEE: $20 semimodern, $25 or $29 modern ($20 or $24 off-season)

ELEVATION: 1,028'

RESTRICTIONS

PETS: On leash only

FIRES: Fire pits only

ALCOHOL: Permitted in campground only

VEHICLES: Michigan Recreation Passport required (see page 8); 2 vehicles/site

OTHER: 6 people/site; 14-day stay limit

it. (For that, check out the Metamora–Hadley State Recreation Area.) It's at least a mile from the campground to the park's Heron Lake, but what might be an inconvenience for some is a boon for others. You would be amazed at how many of the thousands who visit the park aren't even aware there is a campground here, which is surprising because it's not a small campground.

All told, McGinnis Lake has 159 campsites on five different loops. Of those, 144 are designated modern sites, meaning they have electrical service and modern restrooms. The remaining 15 semimodern sites (that is, sites without electricity) are located on the Aspen Loop. These might seem like the best bet for tent campers. The loop, however, is wide open—the campsites back up to some trees, but there are precious few trees between sites, and that can make it feel like you're camping in a field. The modern sites, with their fancy electrical hookups and paved parking areas, are more expensive, but many of these are located on quieter loops, cushioned from neighbors by the surrounding forest. The Trillium and Oak Loops offer a nice sense of privacy—and both are connected by short paths with the park's stunning 6.4-mile Holly-Wilderness Trail.

Because the park is so close to urban life, it's not uncommon for weekends to host a party crowd from time to time. The park is generally good about enforcing quiet hours, but be aware that it can be uncomfortable if you are cursed with inconsiderate neighbors. (Another reason to reserve a modern site.)

The campground, and the entire park, has a remote feeling—which is surprising when you consider that one side of the park butts up against Dixie Highway. When you trace Dixie south on a map, ignoring the M-24 nonsense, you see that the road is an extension of Woodward Avenue. This was once the old American Indian trail that connected the Detroit River with settlements on the Saginaw River. Back in 1831, the French social observer Alexis de Tocqueville and his traveling companion wanted to explore the wilds of America. This brought them to Detroit, where they hired horses. In Pontiac they hired a guide, and with that they headed into the uncivilized frontier.

Tocqueville describes the country in his essay "Two Weeks in the Wilderness." He tells of small lakes "like a sheet of silver beneath the forest foliage," of a ground "intersected by hills and valleys," and of a "deep peace and an uninterrupted silence" (from *Two Essays on America*, translated by Gerald Bevan). Unfortunately, he also predicted that European settlers would eventually arrive, clearing the forest to make way for homesteads and farm fields. The best part of Holly Recreation Area—a bit of country through which Tocqueville surely passed on his way to Saginaw Bay—is that in some small way the park preserves that sense of deep peace and uninterrupted silence.

Of course, traffic can be heard dully humming in the background, and during the day the beach is packed with families playing in the water, but if you're looking to experience a bit of the primeval forest, a night at Holly Recreation Area is a good place to start.

Holly Recreation Area: McGinnis Lake Campground

GETTING THERE

From Exit 93 off I-75 west of Clarkston, head north on Dixie Highway for 7.2 miles; then make a sharp right onto Grange Hall Road. In 0.4 mile, make a slight right onto McGinnis Road; in another 0.8 mile, turn left (north) to reach the campground, 0.2 mile farther.

From I-75 between metro Detroit and Flint, take the Holly exit (Exit 101) for Grange Hall Road, and head east about 2.5 miles. Then make a slight right onto McGinnis Road, and proceed as above.

GPS COORDINATES: N42° 48.994' W83° 31.515'

⚲ Lake Hudson Recreation Area Campground

Beauty ★★★★ Privacy ★★★ Spaciousness ★★★★★ Quiet ★★★★ Security ★★★★ Cleanliness ★★★★★

The recreation area is nearly 2,800 acres of gently rolling meadows and woods surrounding a warm inland lake.

Lake Hudson is the most southerly campground in this book. In Lenawee County, the park entrance is just 9 miles from the Ohio border. This part of the state fits with many people's notion of the Midwest—miles of farmland and long drives broken up by small towns that the interstates have largely bypassed. And while northern Ohio and southern Michigan do not have the endless cornfield vistas of Iowa or Nebraska, the miles of open acreage broken up by distant hedgerows of trees and the occasional creek are just as uneventful to the uninitiated.

Many destinations (at least, here in the Great Lake State) dispel this stereotype, but Lake Hudson is in the heart of it. The park consists of nearly 2,800 acres of gently rolling meadows and woods that encircle a warm inland lake. It is far from the state's main transportation arteries—8 miles from US 127, a back-road highway that connects Lansing and Jackson to the north with points south. The nearest town with a significant population is Adrian, 15 miles to the east. Once you leave the highways, it's all country driving.

The campground is nearly 2 miles from the park entrance; the road passes through open meadows and areas forested with white birch, box elder, and mixed hardwoods. Along the way are turnoffs for the boat launch and the beach area. The campground is semimodern, meaning that most sites have electricity, but that's the extent of the modern amenities. The

Lake Hudson is lovely even on a cloudy day.

Photo: Corey Seeman

KEY INFORMATION

CONTACT: Michigan DNR–Lake Hudson Recreation Area, 517-445-2265, michigan.gov/lakehudson; reservations: 800-447-2757, midnrreservations.com

OPEN: April–November

SITES: 50

EACH SITE HAS: Picnic table and fire pit

ASSIGNMENT: Online or by phone

REGISTRATION: At park office

AMENITIES: Electricity, well water, and vault toilets

PARKING: At sites

NIGHTLY FEE: $20

ELEVATION: 865'

RESTRICTIONS

PETS: On leash only

FIRES: Fire pits or in waist-high stoves in the picnic area only

ALCOHOL: Permitted

VEHICLES: Michigan Recreation Passport required (see page 8); 2 vehicles/site

OTHER: 6 people/site; 15-day stay limit

campground is divided into two sections—east and west—each with 25 campsites. Each section has a vault toilet, and they share a hand-pump well and a Dumpster.

There are few trees, and privacy was apparently not a factor when the sites were laid out. Thick brush does a great job of blocking views of campers on each side, but the view directly across is unobstructed. The campsites in the east section, specifically the even-numbered sites, back up to each other and offer the least in the way of privacy. Sites 10 and 14 are practically one open area. And sites such as 27 are so exposed that it's hard to imagine camping here without a trailer for privacy and an expansive awning for shade. For tent campers, many sites are open to the sun all day, which can make for an uncomfortable stay in the summer.

The west section has the choicest spots to pitch a tent. Sites 37 and 38 are wooded, more secluded, and right on the water. But even the sites here, away from the water, seem to offer more privacy.

The park's relatively flat geography and remote location make it a great spot for amateur astronomers. In 1993, the state legislature designated Lake Hudson as Michigan's first dark-sky preserve. (Michigan was the first state to set up a preserve like this on public land.) The lights of Detroit and Toledo are distant distractions on the horizon and are easily ignored when the Milky Way stretches across the night sky. Wherever lighting is necessary within the park, it is directed at the ground and shielded (operated with motion detectors, if possible).

It's not just astronomers who appreciate a dark night. As more and more of the planet is covered with artificial light, the night skies have grown noticeably dim, and not just in urban areas. City lights reflected off the atmosphere create a glare that obscures stars and other nighttime phenomena miles away. Just as many campers head to state parks and other campgrounds to escape the noise of civilization, so finding a dark-sky preserve such as this offers campers an opportunity to escape the visual noise of the city and suburbs as well.

Of course, overnight park visitors will need light. A late-night jog to the vault toilet without a flashlight is ill-advised, and the fire pits aren't just for show. But visitors are asked to keep the use of lights at night to a minimum.

Day users come to the recreation area for Lake Hudson itself. The park has a decent beach, picnic area, and volleyball nets. The water gets warm in the summer and makes for great swimming. The day-use area is more than a mile away around a bend in the lake, and even on busy days it is out of sight for most campers. Spring, summer, and fall find anglers trolling the 600-acre lake, mainly looking to land muskies—the lake reputably has some of the largest around—but bluegill, largemouth and smallmouth bass, and walleye are not uncommon.

Gently rolling meadows, wetlands, and woods are perfect habitats for waterfowl, pheasants and turkeys, deer, and small game. Hunters make good use of the land in season.

July is the busiest camping season. May and the first half of June, as well as mid- to late August, are your best bets for finding one of the two or three really choice sites. Reserve online or by phone, but know that there's hardly a time when you'll find the campground completely full.

Lake Hudson Recreation Area Campground

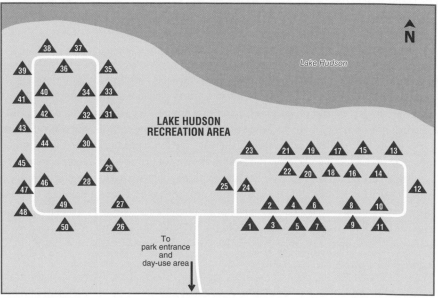

GETTING THERE

From the west: Take Exit 142 off I-94 onto US 127 South. Continue south about 30 miles, and turn left (east) onto M-34 (Main Street/West Carleton Road) in Hudson. Continue 6.5 miles, turn right (south) onto M-156 (Morey Highway), and drive about 1.5 miles to the signed park entrance, on your right. In about 2.1 miles, turn left (south) to reach the campground, about 0.6 mile farther.

From the east: Take US 23 to Exit 5 in Albion. From the northbound exit, take the third exit off the traffic circle, heading right (west), onto US 223; from the southbound exit, take the first exit off the traffic circle, again heading right (west), onto US 223. In about 21 miles, turn left (west) onto M-34. In 5 miles, bear left to continue south on M-34; then, in another 2 miles, bear right to continue west on M-34 (West Carleton Road). In 3.9 miles, turn left (south) on M-156 (Morey Highway). Drive about 1.5 miles to the park entrance, on your right, and proceed as above.

GPS COORDINATES: N41° 49.482' W84° 15.576'

Pinckney Recreation Area:
CROOKED LAKE AND BLIND LAKE CAMPGROUNDS

Beauty ★★★ Privacy ★★★★ Spaciousness ★★★★★ Quiet ★★★★★ Security ★★★★ Cleanliness ★★★★

You can pitch your tent on a wooded rise overlooking Blind Lake. In the evening, campers can relax to the sound of peepers in the nearby wetlands.

Northwest of Ann Arbor sits a rugged playground: the 11,000 acres of Pinckney Recreation Area. The park incorporates part of a larger terminal moraine area, which was formed at the end of a glacier—the soil is sandy and gravelly, the park is full of steep wooded hills, and the depressions in between them have become ponds and lakes. Taking full advantage of this unique terrain, the park has 26 miles of trails climbing in and around (and up and over) these hills. Pinckney Recreation Area and the neighboring Waterloo Recreation Area attract thousands of hikers and mountain bikers annually, and avid backpackers come for southern Michigan's longest hike, the 36-mile Waterloo–Pinckney Trail, which was created to offer overnight hikers a multiday trip. The park is also popular with anglers who appreciate the dozens of small lakes and ponds.

In addition, the recreation area has three campgrounds. The one modern campground, Bruin Lake, with 186 sites, is the largest and most popular. Though relatively spacious and wooded, the sites are plotted like a parking lot, not to mention this campground stays very busy all summer—it's visited not only by campers but also by folks looking to enjoy Bruin Lake for the day.

Silver Lake is your starting point for hikes throughout Pinckney Recreation Area.

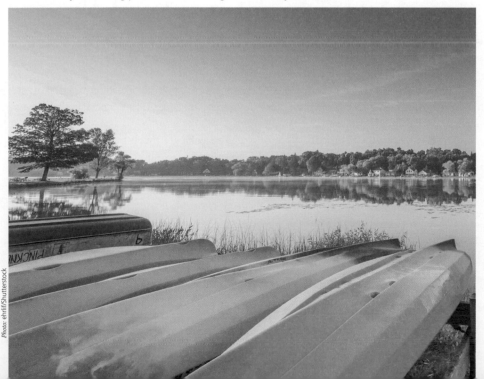

KEY INFORMATION

CONTACT: Michigan DNR–Pinckney Recreation Area, 734-426-4913, michigan.gov/pinckney; reservations: 800-447-2757, midnrreservations.com

OPEN: Blind Lake, year-round; Crooked Lake, April–November

SITES: Blind Lake, 10; Crooked Lake, 25

EACH SITE HAS: Picnic table and fire pit

ASSIGNMENT: Online or by phone

REGISTRATION: At park office, or self-register if office is closed

AMENITIES: Water and vault toilets

PARKING: Crooked Lake, at sites only; must park at Potawatomi Trailhead for Blind Lake sites

NIGHTLY FEE: $17

ELEVATION: 922'

RESTRICTIONS

PETS: On leash only

FIRES: Fire pits only

ALCOHOL: Permitted

VEHICLES: Michigan Recreation Passport required (see page 8); 2 vehicles/site at Crooked Lake; no vehicles at Blind Lake

OTHER: 6 people/site; 15-day stay limit at Crooked Lake; 1-night stay limit at Blind Lake

For a more secluded retreat, look for the 25 sites on Crooked Lake and the 10 sites on Blind Lake. The lack of warm showers and flush toilets keeps the less adventurous crowds away from these rustic campgrounds.

The sites on Blind Lake are located along the Potawatomi Trail, and campers have to either hike or bike into their camps. These sites are spaced with privacy in mind, and even the closest (2 and 3) have an obstructed sight line. Site 3 may be Pinckney's most desirable; you can pitch your tent on a wooded rise overlooking Blind Lake. In the evening campers can relax to the sound of peepers in the nearby wetlands.

The Potawatomi Trail makes a 17-mile loop through the eastern two-thirds of the park. Beginning at the parking lot in Silver Lake, it cuts a path west and north through dense woods, leg-burning hills, and sections of wheel-grabbing sand. Mountain bikers are supposed to ride clockwise, while hikers walk the loop counterclockwise. This way, hikers don't have to keep looking over their shoulders, and mountain bikers only have to worry about running into folks on foot around hidden corners.

On Saturday nights in the summer, the campground at Blind Lake is often full. You can reserve online or register at the park office before you hike in. Campers park at the day-use area and hike about 7 miles to the campground.

The 25 sites on the northeast shore of Crooked Lake are much more accessible. Many sites near the water have no trees for shade. Some sites have no natural dividing line and offer no privacy. There are, however, some real gems tucked in the woods away from the water. The campground has a boat launch and a fishing pier, which means anglers and boaters will keep the area busy on weekends. All told, choosing a site away from the water will greatly improve your stay. If water is a must, sites 21 and 22 are wooded and on the lake.

Campers will find the best sites on the middle loop. Site 13 offers plenty of privacy, and sites 9 and 11 have room to spread out. I'm also fond of sites 1–4. These are farthest from the water on grassy lots with shade.

The drive from the park office to the campground is 1.5 miles. When you register (or self-register after-hours) at the office, they ask that you first go out and pick a site. On a busy

Pinckney Recreation Area: Crooked Lake Campground

Pinckney Recreation Area: Blind Lake Campground

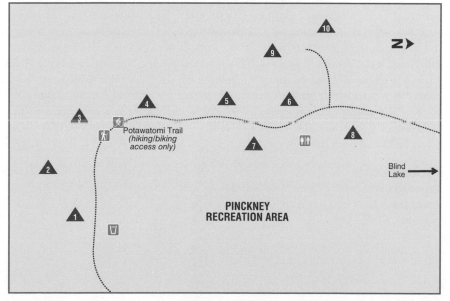

evening, campers have driven out to the campground, found a site, and returned to the office only to find that the site they selected was registered to another camper while they were out looking, someone they must have passed along the road. Register online ahead of time if you can. Otherwise, be prepared to leave a bag at your chosen site so that the next unfortunate camper doesn't come right behind you to register the same site.

Mountain bikers know Pinckney Recreation Area has some of the best trails in southeast Michigan: no rail-to-trail paved pathways here. This is New England–style singletrack. Rolling terrain, some tight technical areas, and a variety of loops keep it interesting. Unique to these trails are the sandy sections, which seem to pop up in the most unfortunate places (such as at the bottom of a hill, around a tight corner, or on a straightaway when you're looking for speed).

For hikers, the trails offer much more than a day of walking. The Waterloo–Pinckney Trail alone crosses 36 miles, connecting the park with the Waterloo Recreation Area. (This trail starts in Waterloo for hikers walking west to east. See the profile for Green Lake Campground, page 24, for more information.) Hikers looking for a shorter walk in the woods can tackle the 5-mile loop out and around Crooked Lake or the 2-mile Silver Lake Trail. There are others as well, all accessed from the parking area on Silver Lake.

Silver Lake also offers better swimming than campers will find at Crooked Lake. And for folks who appreciate the amenities of a modern campground, there are flush toilets at Silver Lake, and campers can always drive over to Bruin Lake Campground for a hot shower.

GETTING THERE

The starting point for adventure at Pinckney begins on Silver Hill Road. From Island Lake Road in Dexter, take Dexter–Pinckney Road north for 3.6 miles; then turn left (west) onto North Territorial Road. In 2.3 miles, turn right (north) onto Dexter Townhall Road. In 1.1 miles, turn left into the park on Silver Hill Road.

From US 23 in Whitmore Lake, take Exit 49: from the northbound exit, take the third exit off the traffic circle, heading right (west) onto North Territorial Road; from the southbound exit, turn right (west) onto North Territorial Road. In about 10.6 miles, turn right (north) onto Dexter Townhall Road. In 1.1 miles, turn left into the park on Silver Hill Road.

To reach Crooked Lake, continue 0.6 mile north on Silver Hill Road from the park entrance; then turn left at the fork, continue another 0.9 mile, and make another left to reach the campground, 0.2 mile farther. To reach the day-use parking area and the Potawatomi Trailhead, from which you'll need to hike to reach Blind Lake, continue 0.7 mile north on Silver Hill Road from the park entrance.

GPS COORDINATES:
Crooked Lake N42° 25.308' W83° 58.752'
Blind Lake N42° 24.730' W84° 01.208'

4

Port Crescent State Park Campground

Beauty ★★★★★ Privacy ★★★ Spaciousness ★★★★★ Quiet ★★★★ Security ★★★★★ Cleanliness ★★★★★

This quiet campground sits adjacent to 3 miles of sandy Lake Huron beach.

If you picture the flow of tourists surging north during the summer months as a river, the Thumb region of Michigan is a quiet eddy, off by itself. Bypassed by major highways, this part of the state has its own rhythms as the current takes the great mass of warm-weather travelers north and west, to Lake Michigan, to Grand Traverse Bay, to Mackinac. In a way, this makes no sense. The Thumb is surrounded by Lake Huron (the second largest of the Great Lakes), and the Saginaw Bay offers warm, shallow water; sandbars that go out forever; and miles of beautiful beaches — all just an hour or so from the state's largest urban center.

What might be disappointing for a struggling business in Port Austin, however, is great news for campers. Two state parks sit on Lake Huron near the tip of the Thumb: Albert E. Sleeper and Port Crescent. With more than 200 sites, Albert Sleeper is the larger of the two, and it's not a bad place for camping. It sits back from the water, on the other side of the highway, in fact, and campers access the park beach by way of a pedestrian bridge. The Port Crescent campground, however, has almost half the number of campsites as its neighbor and is tucked in along the water. While the former has a fine reputation with campers, many of whom return year after year, I've developed a preference for the latter.

The park straddles the Pinnebog River. The day-use area, west of the river, has plenty of parking for beachgoers. There's a fitness trail and a fun day-use hiking trail. East of the river,

Dune grass contrasts with sandy beaches at Port Crescent State Park.

Photo: ehrlif/Shutterstock

KEY INFORMATION

CONTACT: Michigan DNR–Port Crescent State Park, 989-738-8663, michigan.gov /portcrescent; reservations: 800-447-2757, midnrreservations.com

OPEN: Mid-April–October

SITES: 142

EACH SITE HAS: Picnic table and fire pit

ASSIGNMENT: Online or by phone

REGISTRATION: At park office

AMENITIES: Electricity, water, hot showers, modern restrooms, and pit toilets

PARKING: At sites

NIGHTLY FEE: $33 electric, $45 full hookup ($25 or $29 off-season)

ELEVATION: 590'

RESTRICTIONS

PETS: On leash only

FIRES: Fire pits only

ALCOHOL: Permitted

VEHICLES: Michigan Recreation Passport required (see page 8); 2 vehicles/site

OTHER: 6 people/site; 15-day stay limit

next to the Old Pinnebog River Channel, is the campground. All told, the state park has 640 acres on Lake Huron.

The campground loop, with its 142 sites, is laid out lengthwise, so there are plenty of spaces to pitch a tent. The sites along the water, however, are the best of the lot. The campground is, of course, very sandy, but campsites are tucked into the woods that skirt the beach. The view from the campground faces the northwest. Because the earth executes its annual tilt every summer, the sun's arc shifts northward, and the region's late evening sunsets are perfectly spotted for campers on the inside shore of the Thumb.

The park sits on the former site of Port Crescent, a boom town that cashed in on the region's lumber. It's hard to imagine now, but there was once a schoolhouse and a church here, as well as a hotel and a tavern. Sawmills lined the Pinnebog River, processing logs floating out from the interior. All that's left today is a bridge and the chimney monument, once part of a large brick sawmill.

The lumber boom that gave birth to the village of Port Crescent played an important role in the history of the region. Few people today remember the Fire of 1871, which destroyed millions of acres in Michigan. That story has been overshadowed by two other fires that started at the same time—the Peshtigo Fire in Wisconsin and the Chicago Fire (for which Mrs. O'Leary's unfortunate cow was to be the scapegoat). The Fire of 1871 would be the most destructive conflagration in Michigan history, but for the Thumb region it was just a dry run for the Great Thumb Fire of 1881.

In the intervening years, a wave of settlers moved in and put down roots here. So on September 5, 1881, when hurricane-force winds and high heat pushed a ravenous fire across the Thumb, it not only devoured more than a million acres, but it also killed 282 people and left thousands homeless. In a way, however, these fires helped clear the land for tenacious settlers who continued to come to farm.

Today, the Thumb region of the state depends on its agriculture. Farmers grow navy beans and sugar beets. The Michigan Sugar Company takes these beets and produces the Pioneer and Big Chief brands of sugar. But along the coast, tourism remains a persistent, if not quiet, industry. The arc of M-25 connects the tourist towns of Port Huron, Lexington, Port Austin, Caseville, and Bay City. Port Crescent State Park is close to Port Austin and an easy drive from Caseville (and the ever-growing Cheeseburger in Caseville Festival). With sites close to the water and 3 miles of sandy beach, the park offers a quiet escape, right in the heart of things.

Port Crescent State Park Campground

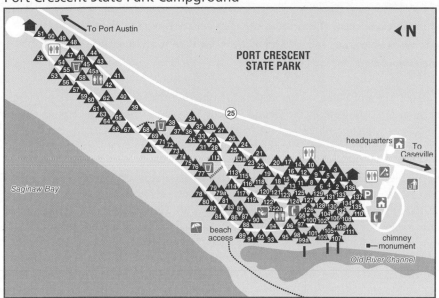

GETTING THERE

M-25 makes a huge arc, tracing the Thumb from Bay City to Port Huron. From points west, take I-75 to Bay City (Exit 162) and follow M-25 east about 65 miles to the signed campground entrance, on your left.

From metro Detroit, take the Imlay City exit (Exit 168) off I-69 and head north on M-53. In about 54 miles, bear left to continue north on Pinnebog Road; then, in another 11.4 miles, turn right (east) onto Kindle Road. In 2 miles, turn left (north) onto McMillan Road and, in another 2 miles, turn right onto Oak Beach Road. In 0.5 mile, turn left (north) onto Kennedy Road, and drive 2.3 miles. Finally, turn right onto M-25 and drive 0.6 mile to the campground entrance, on your left.

GPS COORDINATES: N44° 00.414' W83° 03.100'

5

⛺ Waterloo Recreation Area:
GREEN LAKE CAMPGROUND

Beauty ★★★★ Privacy ★★★ Spaciousness ★★★★★ Quiet ★★★★★ Security ★★★★ Cleanliness ★★★★★

Part of the experience, of course, is engaging with nature, and there's no better way to immerse yourself in the heart of Waterloo than to pitch camp in the park's rustic campground.

The 20,000 acres of Waterloo Recreation Area make it the largest state park in the Lower Peninsula. The park features the Gerald E. Eddy Discovery Center, where people come to learn about the local ecology, and the Waterloo Farm Museum, which is operated by the Waterloo Area Historical Society. Though the park shares many traits with the neighboring Pinckney Recreation Area—it has two modern campgrounds (to Pinckney's one); a swimming beach; and trails for hiking, biking, and horseback riding—Waterloo places more of an emphasis on interpreting the region's natural and human history for visitors.

Part of the experience, of course, is engaging with nature, and there's no better way to immerse yourself in the heart of Waterloo than to pitch camp in the park's rustic Green Lake Campground, which consists of 25 sites on a small loop. Sites overlook the lake on one side and back up to wetlands on the other. Circling a small grassy knoll, many of the sites on the inside are out in the open, exposed both to the elements and to the eyes of nearby campers. Sites on the outside of the loop, however, are nestled in the trees and offer a little more privacy.

Site 8 offers the most seclusion. Surrounded by trees, right on the water, the site is downhill from the main road that runs through the campground. Sites 5 and 6 also sit on the water. The wide, grassy lots have nice overhead coverage from the sun but little privacy.

The first signs of spring emerge at Waterloo Recreation Area.

Photo: Hank Erdmann/Shutterstock

KEY INFORMATION

CONTACT: Michigan DNR–Waterloo Recreation Area, 734-475-8307, michigan.gov/waterloo; reservations: 800-447-2757, midnrreservations.com

OPEN: Early April–November

SITES: 25

EACH SITE HAS: Picnic table and fire pit

ASSIGNMENT: Online or by phone

REGISTRATION: Self-register at campground

AMENITIES: Water and vault toilets

PARKING: At sites

NIGHTLY FEE: $17

ELEVATION: 965'

RESTRICTIONS

PETS: On leash only

FIRES: Fire pits only

ALCOHOL: Permitted

VEHICLES: Michigan Recreation Passport required (see page 8); 2 vehicles/site

OTHER: 6 people/site; 15-day stay limit

Sites 2 and 4, which sit across from these, also enjoy plenty of shade, but when someone decides to crank open a pop-up between you and the water, it will most certainly block the view of the lake.

Waterloo boasts a 5-mile mountain bike loop, but trail planners overlapped the trail with a longer bridle path, and in the past this has made the track unridable. Your best bet is to take your mountain bike next door. The miles of maintained singletrack at Pinckney will not disappoint.

Campers looking for a nice hike in the woods, or through a meadow or around a lake, are in for better luck. A network of nature hikes—14 miles of trails divvied up into seven loops ranging from 0.8 to 5.3 miles—all lead out from the Discovery Center. The Discovery Center draws thousands of visitors every year, including busloads of students. Run as a joint project by the Michigan Department of Natural Resources and the Waterloo Natural History Association, the center sheds light on the region's unique geology and ecology. With its hands-on exhibits and displays and a full complement of programs for kids and families, you'll come away with a head full of knowledge about local birds and their plumage; the hive building of bees; glacial periods, glaciers, and mammoths; Waterloo's trees and flowers; and even a little astronomy.

Among the area's geological peculiarities are its kettle lakes and bogs, part of the glacial influence on southeast Michigan. The bogs here are home to some of the most exotic plants in the state, in particular carnivorous pitcher plants and sundews, as well as wild irises. You might spot some of these when hiking the Bog Trail. Much of this path is on an elevated wooden walkway—no need to worry about returning with wet shoes.

Hikers looking for more than an afternoon stroll, however, will want to take note of the 36-mile Waterloo–Pinckney Trail, which connects Pinckney Recreation Area (to the east, between Pinckney and Dexter) with the Waterloo Recreation Area (to the west, between Waterloo and Chelsea). The trail was designed to offer backpackers a multiday hike in southeast Michigan. Backpackers typically follow the trail west to east, beginning the trek at the modern Portage Lake Campground. A day of hiking brings them to the park's other modern campground at Sugarloaf Lake. Ten miles farther, just before entering the Pinckney portion of the trail, hikers will often spend the night at Green Lake Campground.

The portion of the trail that passes through the Waterloo Recreation Area is quite stunning, and I would recommend taking some time to hike a piece. Along the way, the path passes through woods and marsh, as well as fields that are covered with wildflowers in the summer. It climbs some interesting terrain and comes close to nearly a dozen lakes and ponds. The trail can be especially arresting in the fall, when the foliage begins to change color.

For an appreciation of what it must have been like to come to this area as a settler, head over to the Waterloo Farm Museum. In 1844, Johannes and Fredericka Ruehle moved their children into a log house here, and the museum tells the story of this family and their progeny. For more than a hundred years, the Realy family—*Realy* is the Americanized spelling of the German *Ruehle*—farmed this land, and their story sheds light on what life was like for many families across Michigan. From the farmhouse to the bakehouse and plenty of other structures in between, this is a great place to spend a few hours.

Waterloo Recreation Area: Green Lake Campground

GETTING THERE

From I-94 in Chelsea, take Exit 159 and head north on M-52. The campground entrance is 5.5 miles ahead on your left.

GPS COORDINATES: N42° 21.846' W84° 04.218'

SOUTHWEST MICHIGAN

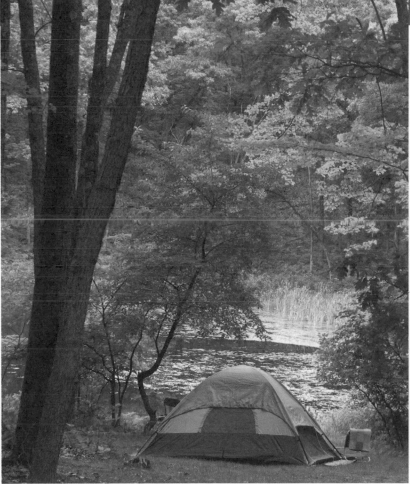

Photo: U.S. Forest Service (public domain)

Highbanks Lake National Forest Campground (see Campground 7, page 31) strikes a nice balance between too developed and too primitive.

6

Fort Custer State Recreation Area Campground

Beauty ★★★ Privacy ★★★★ Spaciousness ★★★ Quiet ★★★ Security ★★★★ Cleanliness ★★★★

More than 20 miles of trails wind through the park's woods for mountain biking, and there are paths for hiking in the summer and snowshoeing, cross-country skiing, and dogsledding in the winter.

By the name you might think that Fort Custer State Recreation Area has some connection to General George Custer. The famed 19th-century general grew up in Monroe, just 100 miles to the east, after all. But the association is just commemorative. Back in 1917, the government built a camp here to train soldiers for World War I. All told, more than 100,000 men made their way through Camp Custer. Later the camp received a promotion and became Fort Custer. In 1971, the portion of the government's property that is now the recreation area was deeded over to the state of Michigan.

The Kalamazoo River flows through Fort Custer State Recreation Area.

Photo: Bill Dolak

KEY INFORMATION

CONTACT: Michigan DNR–Fort Custer Recreation Area, 269-731-4200, michigan.gov /fortcuster; reservations: 800-447-2757, midnrreservations.com

OPEN: Year-round

SITES: 219 modern sites

EACH SITE HAS: Picnic table and fire pit

ASSIGNMENT: Online or by phone

REGISTRATION: Self-register at campground

AMENITIES: Electricity, modern restrooms, and pit toilets

PARKING: At sites

NIGHTLY FEE: $25 ($20 off-season)

ELEVATION: 797'

RESTRICTIONS

PETS: On leash only

FIRES: In fire pits only

ALCOHOL: Not allowed April 1–Labor Day

VEHICLES: Michigan Recreation Passport required (see page 8); 2 vehicles/site

OTHER: 6 people/site; 14-day stay limit

There is still a military presence here: the Fort Custer Army National Guard Reserve site borders the east side of the park. The west side is bounded by the Kalamazoo River. The small town of Augusta is perched just on the other side of the river across from the park's northwest corner.

The river, which has its headwaters southwest of Jackson, flows through Albion, Marshall, and Battle Creek before passing by the recreation area. It continues west and then northwest through Kalamazoo and Allegan, passes between Saugatuck and Douglas, and finally empties into Lake Michigan. The Kalamazoo River Watershed Council organizes Kanoe the Kazoo events all along the river, including a stretch through Augusta and Fort Custer Rec.

The park encompasses more than 3,000 acres, all told. Within this acreage are three lakes with boat launches. One of those, Eagle Lake, has a popular beach and offers concessions in season. All of the lakes are designated as no-wake, so paddlers can enjoy time on the water without the constant whine of motors and relatively smooth water. For visitors who want to paddle and forgot to bring a canoe, the park has a boat rental.

More than 20 miles of trails wind through the park's woods for mountain biking, and there are paths for hiking in the summer and snowshoeing, cross-country skiing, and dog-sledding in the winter. Fishing and hunting are also very popular at Fort Custer.

On a map, the campground looks like two kidneys in the center of the park. Each kidney features a modern bathroom at its center, with vault toilets at the north and south ends for easy nighttime treks to the bathroom. The campground also has swings and a playground. For campers less pleased with the idea of sleeping on the ground, there are several cabins for rent.

Fort Custer is particularly popular because of its accessibility. Located between Battle Creek and Kalamazoo, just north of I-94, it's the perfect destination for a short weekend camping trip for folks in the lower half of the state.

Fort Custer State Recreation Area Campground

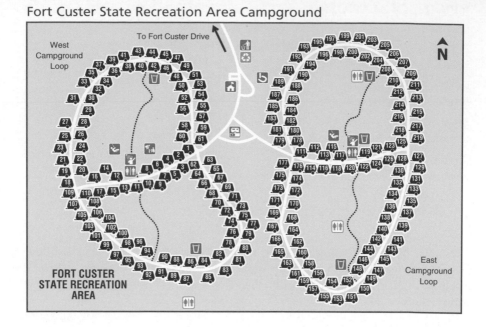

GETTING THERE

From I-94 south of Battle Creek, take Exit 95 north onto Helmer Road. In 3.6 miles, come to a T and turn left (west) onto M-96; then, in 5.8 miles, turn left (south) onto Fort Custer Drive to enter the park. In 1.2 miles, bear left at the fork and drive 0.2 mile to the campground entrance, on your right.

GPS COORDINATES: N42° 19.310' W85° 21.026'

7

Highbank Lake National Forest Campground

Beauty ★★★★ Privacy ★★★★ Spaciousness ★★★ Quiet ★★★★★ Security ★★★★★ Cleanliness ★★★★

The area verily bristles with recreational opportunities.

The Manistee National Forest maintains a handful of campgrounds between the towns of Baldwin and White Cloud, all close to M-37. The Pere Marquette River and several of its tributaries run through this part of the forest, and the area verily bristles with recreational opportunities—camping, hiking, paddling, and fishing, to name a few. Nearby, the North Country Trail winds around rivers and lakes, passing close enough to most of these campgrounds to be connected by short spurs.

Highbank Lake Campground is in good company. To the south, its neighbors are Benton Lake and Nichols Lake Campgrounds; to the east, Shelley Lake Campground; and, just a few miles north, Bowman Bridge Campground (the only one of the lot on the Pere Marquette River). Though all are in close proximity, these campgrounds offer very different camping experiences. While the campground at Nichols Lake seems particularly convenient for RVs—with well-defined packed-gravel spurs and flush and vault toilets—the narrow, rutted drive into the dispersed sites at Shelley Lake would be a tight squeeze for anything bigger than a humble SUV, and the campground doesn't even offer potable water or an outhouse. The campground at Highbank Lake strikes a balance between these two.

As the name suggests, the ground around the lake rises steeply from the water's edge. There's room enough for four campsites right on the lake, but the rest of the campground's

Although there's no official boat launch here, Highbank Lake is a pleasant place to paddle.

Photo: U.S. Forest Service (public domain)

KEY INFORMATION

CONTACT: Huron–Manistee National Forest, Baldwin/White Cloud Ranger District; 231-745-4631, tinyurl.com/highbank

OPEN: Early May–early September

SITES: 9

EACH SITE HAS: Picnic table, fire pit with grill, and lantern post

ASSIGNMENT: First come, first served; no reservations

REGISTRATION: Self-register at campground

AMENITIES: Hand-pumped water and vault toilets

PARKING: At sites

NIGHTLY FEE: $18

ELEVATION: 885'

RESTRICTIONS

PETS: On leash only

FIRES: Fire pits only

ALCOHOL: No stated restrictions; check ahead to confirm

VEHICLES: 2/site

OTHER: 8 people/site; 14-day stay limit

nine sites are spotted on the rise, nestled under a canopy of oak and the occasional maple. Two in particular, sites 7 and 8, are a ways up the hill, requiring campers to park alongside the loop and hike up and in. With only nine sites and no way to make reservations, you take your chances camping here on peak summer weekends.

For tent camping, Highbank proves to be especially equipped. Only a few of these sites can accommodate RVs, and campground facilities include a vault toilet and water from a hand-pump well. But the sloping terrain can present difficulties. Site 1, for example, offers campers great access to the water, but you have to watch the pitch when setting up your tent. It's easy to see how a sudden rainstorm could generate a mini-deluge. Even in good weather, I imagine a poorly planned location would result in campers fighting the roll of gravity throughout the night. (None of these drawbacks, however, would keep me from trying to snag site 1 if it was available.)

In late summer, lying in your tent and listening to the sounds of the forest, you will hear the smack of acorns falling on the carpet of last year's leaves (and your tent, for that matter). Above the lake, ferns cover the forest floor on both sides of the drive in. If you miss the turn for the campground, you will soon find yourself immersed in an intricate web of sandy doubletrack. Make a turn without paying special attention to landmarks, and you will drive around confused until you eventually emerge on some thoroughfare of substance. These Forest Service roads, however, would be nice for an evening walk or to explore with a mountain bike.

For more vigorous exploration of the Manistee National Forest, the North Country Trail (NCT) passes the western edge of Highbank Lake. The campground connects to the trail by way of a 0.5-mile spur that follows the northern edge of the lake. You know you've found the trail when you see the blue-diamond blazes. Mountain bikes are prohibited on this stretch of the NCT, but cyclists will find access open to the trail north of the Bowman Lake Trailhead (near Bowman Bridge Campground) and south of Nichols Lake.

The NCT passes through, or close by, quite a few of the campgrounds listed in this book. That's no coincidence. When complete, the NCT will offer hikers an uninterrupted trail from the Adirondacks in New York to Lake Sakakawea in North Dakota, traversing seven states along the way—including the full lengths of both the Upper and Lower Peninsulas. To create a continuous trail on this scale, developers often work by connecting preexisting paths. Trails that are connected to established networks (the kind with campgrounds) are especially necessary to building a successful thru-hike.

There's no formal boat launch here, just access enough to carry your canoe or small rowboat to the water. At only 20 acres, Highbank Lake might be a bit small for a weekend of cruising, but there are plenty of other lakes to explore by canoe and kayak, and the nearby Pere Marquette River is rightfully one of the state's premier paddling rivers.

Anglers at Highbank Lake pull in plenty of bluegill, panfish, and bass. Just southeast of Highbank Lake is the slightly larger Amaung Lake, which some suggest offers better fishing (it certainly offers more-secluded fishing). Surrounded by national forest, with limited access by road (at best), Amaung defines "off the beaten path." According to national forest maps, Forest Service Road 5561 (the first left off FS 5396 once you've turned off Roosevelt Drive) will take you around to the northern end of the lake. But if you simply walk south on FS 5396 (the road you came in on) for 500 yards past the campground entrance and then plunge southeast cross-country through the woods for several hundred feet, you're sure to stumble upon Amaung.

Highbank Lake National Forest Campground

GETTING THERE

From Baldwin, drive south on M-37 for 9 miles, and turn right (west) onto 15 Mile Road. In 0.5 mile, turn right (northwest) onto Roosevelt Drive; then, in 1.5 miles, turn left onto FS 5396, and follow the signs about 0.7 mile to the campground.

GPS COORDINATES: N43° 46.272' W85° 53.316'

8

⛺ Muskegon State Park:
SOUTH CHANNEL CAMPGROUND

Beauty ★★★★ Privacy ★★★ Spaciousness ★★★★ Quiet ★★★ Security ★★★★ Cleanliness ★★★★★

Here you find quiet woods, soaring dunes, and some of the most beautiful beaches on Lake Michigan.

The Muskegon River begins in Houghton Lake near the center of the Lower Peninsula. It flows over 200 miles southwest to empty into Muskegon Lake, tracing a line on the map like a convulsing snake. Bound on either side by the path carved out by a more ancient river, today's river winds back and forth, making tight turns and leaving a wake of oxbow lakes along the way. The river connects to Lake Michigan by way of a shipping channel at the west end of Muskegon Lake.

The city of Muskegon is situated along the south shore of Muskegon Lake. North of the shipping channel, Muskegon Lake is separated from the Great Lake by a dune-covered peninsula. As it curves inward, it also forms a small bay, Snug Harbor. The Muskegon State Park consists of this peninsula and a good stretch of property north along Lake Michigan.

Like many cities in the postindustrial Midwest, Muskegon has struggled economically. In recent years there have been concerted efforts to address issues of urban blight—abandoned cars, vacant buildings, graffiti—and a lot of progress has been made. The park across the water, however, seems untouched by the development, decline, and rebuilding of the city. Here you find quiet woods, soaring dunes, and some of the most beautiful beaches on Lake Michigan.

The park was created in 1923. The property was once owned by Ryerson Hill and Company, which operated a lumber mill on Snug Harbor. The site was purchased by the state,

A rainbow soars over Lake Michigan at Muskegon State Park.

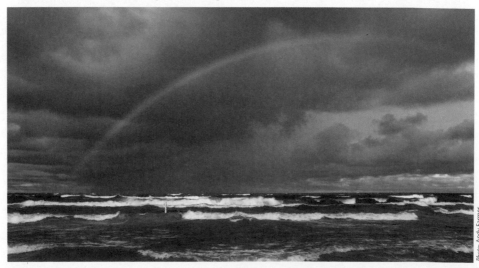

Photo: Andy Farmer

KEY INFORMATION

CONTACT: Muskegon State Park, 231-744-3480, michigan.gov/muskegon; reservations: 800-447-2757, midnrreservations.com

OPEN: Late May–late October

SITES: 139 semimodern

EACH SITE HAS: Picnic table and fire pit

ASSIGNMENT: Online or by phone

REGISTRATION: At park office

AMENITIES: Electricity, well water, and vault toilets

PARKING: At sites

NIGHTLY FEE: $33 for 20/30-amp sites, $37 for 50-amp sites ($25 or $29 off-season)

ELEVATION: 600'

RESTRICTIONS

PETS: On leash only

FIRES: In fire pits only

ALCOHOL: Permitted in campground only

VEHICLES: Michigan Recreation Passport required (see page 8); 2 vehicles/site

OTHER: 6 people/site; 14-day stay limit

and for a couple of years the Civilian Conservation Corps worked to create a park. The most visible reminder of the CCC's contribution was a log blockhouse located in the north end of the park. Built on a high point, the blockade offered visitors a scenic overview of the dunes, Lake Michigan, and Lake Muskegon. The original blockhouse burned down in the 1960s, and it was replaced with the replica that stands there today.

There are two campgrounds at Muskegon State Park. At the north end of the park is the Lake Michigan Campground, with 105 semimodern sites. At the south end of the park, facing Muskegon Lake, is the South Channel Campground—this is the campground highlighted here.

The sites at South Channel have electricity, and the campground has modern restrooms, but aside from these amenities, the place has a rustic feel: sites are sandy, and the trees and grass are low, like you'd expect on a dune. There are campsites that overlook the water—like sites 24, 25, 28, 30, 32, and 33 on the first loop, and sites 110–113 on the second loop. Three large sites have great water access and views—144, 146, and 147—but these also come with a scant amount of shade and very little privacy.

Aside from Memorial Drive, which enters the park from the east, the main road (the only road) in the park is Scenic Drive. The two campgrounds are situated at the north and south ends of this road. For exploring, your best bet is to keep off the roads and take to the park's extensive hiking trails. The Devil's Kitchen Trail, which begins near those later campsites (143 and 145), winds through the dunes, by the site of what was once Old Bay Mills Village overlooking Snug Harbor. These trails connect to others, and ambitious hikers can make their way to the blockhouse and the northern sections of the park.

Most campers, however, use the campground as a base camp for a weekend spent on Lake Michigan. This might mean putting a boat into Muskegon Lake and heading out to the big water. Or they head out in the morning to the beach and public bathhouse and spend the day swimming.

GETTING THERE

From US 31 northeast of Muskegon, take Moses J. Jones Parkway west about 1 mile until it becomes M-120. In 1.5 miles, turn left on Lake Avenue; then, in 0.6 mile, curve right

Muskegon State Park: South Channel Campground (Loop 1)

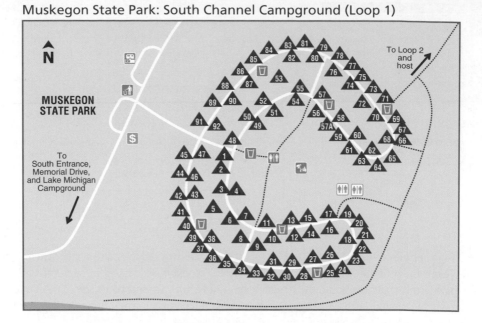

Muskegon State Park: South Channel Campground (Loop 2)

onto Center Street and, in 0.1 mile, turn left (west) onto Ruddiman Drive, which becomes Memorial Drive. In 5.3 miles, turn left onto Scenic Drive and follow it 1.5 miles south to the South Channel Campground entrance, on your right.

GPS COORDINATES: N43° 14.011' W86° 19.926'

9

Pines Point National Forest Campground

Beauty ★★★★★ Privacy ★★★★ Spaciousness ★★★★★ Quiet ★★★★★ Security ★★★★★
Cleanliness ★★★★★

The place is busy on hot summer weekends, as families spend whole days floating around and around—it's nature's own aquatic carousel.

The White River begins north of White Cloud in Newaygo County. Fed by swelling ground-water and numerous streams, it flows past farms and small country towns and through the southern portion of the Manistee National Forest. It's a lively river—not too quick and not too wide—with a childlike tendency to wander. Trace the river's path on a map and you will find it winding, resisting the straight line, and in places nearly looping back on itself. In fact, just southwest of Hesperia, a bend in the river forms a stylized *U*, returning within yards of its original path. The land within this bend is known as Pines Point and gives its name to the greater Pines Point National Forest Recreation Area.

The recreation-area campground has 32 sites on land that sits a bit higher than the nearby White River. Though the campground loosely follows the river's path, only a few sites sit right on the water. The road through the northern part of the campground forms a loop. The choicest sites, in my opinion, are on the right side of the road as you drive into the campground. Sites 7 and 8 directly overlook the water. Though floored with sand and packed dirt, the sites are spacious, level, and free from a lot of undergrowth.

The White River is great for floating, fishing, and paddling.

Photo: U.S. Forest Service (public domain)

KEY INFORMATION

CONTACT: Huron–Manistee National Forest, Baldwin/White Cloud Ranger District, 231-745-4631, tinyurl.com/pinespoint; reservations: 877-444-6777, recreation .gov/camping/campgrounds/233849

OPEN: Early May–early October

SITES: 32

EACH SITE HAS: Picnic table, fire pit with grill, and lantern post

ASSIGNMENT: First come, first served or by reservation

REGISTRATION: Self-register at campground

AMENITIES: Well water, modern restrooms, and vault toilets

PARKING: At sites

NIGHTLY FEE: $18

ELEVATION: 664'

RESTRICTIONS

PETS: On leash only

FIRES: Fire pits only

ALCOHOL: No stated restrictions; check ahead to confirm

VEHICLES: 2/site

OTHER: 8 people/site; 14-day stay limit

It was long known that American Indians inhabited this part of the state. During recent renovations at the campground, artifacts were found, and the area next to site 7 has been cordoned off with a split-rail fence, protecting a native cemetery. In fact, the campground host told me about a young man who, a few weeks before my visit, found a spearhead while playing down by the river. This kind of thing is certainly not unheard of in western Michigan, but the stories are not as common as they once were.

On the main loop, you will find sites 10–28. Campers access the river by way of a path that runs between sites 13 and 15. Sites along the river here are nice, but those along the back side of the loop don't fill up as fast and offer more seclusion. As at many national forest recreation areas, the facilities here are top-notch. The campgrounds feature modern restrooms. Sometimes a fancy flush toilet is all it takes to get a reluctant camper excited to spend a weekend in the woods.

Anglers know the White River as a high-quality fly-fishing river—the kind of place you congratulate yourself for discovering. It is Michigan's southernmost trout stream, and many consider it one of the state's best-kept secrets. Fed by cold springs, the water is not overly warmed by a string of dams, and that keeps it at a temperature that allows certain fisheries to thrive. The salmon and trout populations are relatively strong, and the right season offers impressive runs of steelhead.

Hikers have a few options at Pines Point. Old maps and guidebooks make mention of the White River Trail, which is said to follow the river for 12 miles, but I've not met anyone in recent years who's been able to pick up on the trailhead. The land south and west of the campground, however, is incorporated into the descriptively named White River Semiprimitive Nonmotorized Recreation Area. You'll find a map for the area at the campground. A great number of the U.S. Forest Service roads are open to foot traffic only, and hikers more familiar with the White River SNRA tell me that a trail near the river can be found a little more than a mile south of the campground at FS 9364. This isn't a well-maintained trail with clear blazes, however, so unless you're OK with getting tangled up or lost, I'd stick with the roads.

The point itself is a popular day-use picnic area (a visit to Pines Point for noncampers costs $6 for each vehicle). Walk the trail down to the point from the parking lot, and you immediately understand how this area got its name. The earth is coated in rust-red needles, and at eye level all you see are trunks. Look up and you feel dwarfed by towering pines. According to folks whose families have come here for generations, campers made their way here long before the national forest installed a formal campground, from places such as Grand Rapids and Muskegon, to pitch tents alongside the river. It's easy to see why.

The loop of the river is the picnic area's biggest draw. Kids can toss an inner tube into the river on one side of the loop, float for 30–40 minutes, and arrive back at the picnic area, just feet from where they put in. The place is busy on hot summer weekends as families spend whole days floating around and around—it's nature's own aquatic carousel.

The river provides recreation for more than just anglers and warm-weather tubers. There are close to 33 miles of excellent paddling on White River from Hesperia to where the water drains into White Lake in Whitehall. An easy 3-hour float can be had by putting in upstream in Hesperia and taking out at Pines Point.

Pines Point National Forest Campground

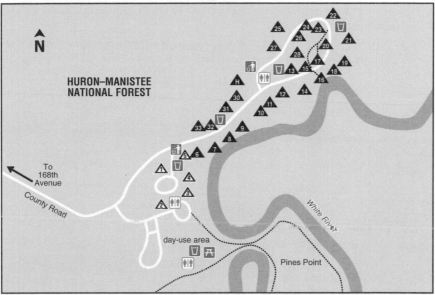

GETTING THERE

From the intersection of M-20 and South Division Street/North Maple Island Road in Hesperia, drive west on M-20 and, in 2 miles, turn left onto 192nd Avenue. Continue south for 1 mile, and turn right onto Garfield Road; then drive west for 3 miles, and turn left (south) onto 168th Avenue. In 1.5 miles, turn left (east) onto County Road and follow it 1.4 miles until it dead-ends at the campground entrance.

GPS COORDINATES: N43° 31.812' W86° 07.020'

10

⛺ P. J. Hoffmaster State Park Campground

Beauty ★★★★ Privacy ★★★ Spaciousness ★★★★ Quiet ★★★★ Security ★★★★ Cleanliness ★★★★★

Each section of the park has its trails, but the best hikes begin close to the Gillette Visitor Center.

Grand Haven is a popular vacation spot. A quaint boardwalk lined with shops and restaurants leads along the Grand River out to Lake Michigan, where a pierhead juts out topped by an inner light and an outer lighthouse. It's no wonder crowds flock here in the summer. South of the lighthouse are a beach and Grand Haven State Park. The views of Lake Michigan from the state park campground are excellent. Unfortunately, the campground is a paved parking lot surrounded by beach sand. There's not a single place to pitch a tent, even if the pavement wasn't 200° in the summer sun. It's like camping in a Walmart parking lot—with more sand.

Tent campers will want to forego the city-bound state park for something quieter, a spot with a bit of cushion under the ground cloth, so to speak. They'll want to head north

A staircase leads to a wide, sandy beach on Lake Michigan at P. J. Hoffmaster State Park.

Photo: ehrlif/Shutterstock

KEY INFORMATION

CONTACT: P. J. Hoffmaster State Park,
231-798-3711, michigan.gov/hoffmaster;
reservations: 800-447-2757,
midnrreservations.com

OPEN: Early April–mid-October

SITES: 297

EACH SITE HAS: Picnic table and fire pit

ASSIGNMENT: Online or by phone

REGISTRATION: At park office

AMENITIES: Electricity, well water,
and vault toilets

PARKING: At sites

NIGHTLY FEE: $33 for 20/30-amp sites, $37
for 50-amp sites ($25 or $29 off-season)

ELEVATION: 594'

RESTRICTIONS

PETS: On leash only

FIRES: In fire pits only

ALCOHOL: Permitted in campground only

VEHICLES: Michigan Recreation Passport
required (see page 8); 2 vehicles/site

OTHER: 6 people/site; 14-day stay limit

4 miles to P. J. Hoffmaster State Park, with its acres of forested dunes and its miles of amazing beach.

Hoffmaster State Park can be divided into three sections. The northern third of the park holds the campground—a 297-site campground (293 modern, 4 semimodern) with modern restrooms and play areas for the kids. The central third of the park has a large parking lot with easy access to the water for beachgoers. There's a place to change into a bathing suit before you hit the water, showers to rinse off after, and restrooms. The southern third of the park is for nature lovers. A huge portion of this section of the park is dedicated quiet space. Here you'll find the Gillette Visitor Center (gillettenature.org) and trails that traverse the various stages of dune ecology—from the open sand and grasses closest the lake to the rich forest of beech and hemlock found farther inland.

Compared with a lot of the campgrounds featured in this book, a nearly-300-site campground might seem a bit overwhelming. There are certainly a lot of people here during the high season, but the campground is nestled into the woods and split into two smaller loops by Little Black Creek. Sites are spacious and though there is not as much privacy as some desire, campers are not stacked up close to each other. For what privacy there is, I recommend those sites along the southern edge of the campground, such as 82 and 84 or the odd-numbered sites from 39 to 61.

Little Black Creek eventually flows down to Lake Michigan, and trails from both sides of the campground will take you there as well. Closer to the water, a trail that parallels the shoreline runs from one end of the park to the other. A nice day activity would be to hike from the campground down to the trails that lead back into the park and the visitor center.

There are trails that make loops through each section of the park, but the best hikes begin close to the Gillette Visitor Center, which is run by the Gillette Nature Association. This group of dedicated staff and volunteers brings the park's natural assets into clear focus with interpretive exhibits, educational opportunities, guided hikes, and more. There's an engaging nature center on the site and a gift shop that helps support the park. The trails in the southern portion of the park wind around and over steep hills, through shady forest. There's a dune overlook and plenty of interpretive signage for an informed walk.

Driftwood on the beach gives the impression of a spooky sea creature.

P. J. Hoffmaster State Park Campground

GETTING THERE

From US 31 north of Grand Haven, take the exit for East Pontaluna Road and follow it west. In about 2.7 miles, when East Pontaluna reaches the park boundary, it curves north and becomes Lake Harbor Road. The signed campground entrance is on your left, about 0.3 mile from the curve.

GPS COORDINATES: N43° 08.209' W86° 16.114'

⛺ Tubbs Lake
State Forest Campgrounds

Beauty ★★★★ Privacy ★★★★ Spaciousness ★★★★★ Quiet ★★★★ Security ★★★★ Cleanliness ★★★★★

Accessed by a narrow strip of land that passes through cattails, purple loosestrifes, and pickerelweed, Tubbs Island is wonderfully secluded.

Early in the 1900s, a beaver dam first gave the Martiny Chain of Lakes in northeastern Mecosta County their shape. In 1955, the Michigan Department of Natural Resources made the flooding more or less permanent with the construction of Winchester Dam. The dam raised water levels 8 feet, creating a chain of eight interconnected lakes: Big Evans, Manake, Saddlebag, Bullhead, Boom, Dogfish, Lost, and Tubbs. (The tally of lakes varies, depending on who's counting. The number gets confused by people who include Pretty Lake and Diamond Lake in the mix.)

Most of these small lakes are only 25–30 feet deep, and the places where they connect are shallow and surrounded by wetlands. On Tubbs Lake in particular, the overall shallowness is a boon, the waters providing a home to a stand of wild rice. This plant, which was much used by American Indians, grows only in the Great Lakes region of the country, but most stands are found in the Upper Peninsula, northern Wisconsin, and Minnesota. In recent years, faculty from Ferris State University in nearby Big Rapids have led a four-day

Tubbs Lake offers campers a sense of peace and quiet, as well as great fishing.

Photo: Urpolski/Shutterstock

KEY INFORMATION

CONTACT: Mecosta County Parks, 989-382-7158, mecostacountyparks.com/tubbslake.html

OPEN: April–mid-October

SITES: 33

EACH SITE HAS: Picnic table and fire pit

ASSIGNMENT: First come, first served; no reservations

REGISTRATION: Self-register at campground

AMENITIES: Hand-pumped water and vault toilets

PARKING: At sites

NIGHTLY FEE: $18

ELEVATION: 1,011'

RESTRICTIONS

PETS: On leash only

FIRES: Fire pits only

ALCOHOL: Permitted

VEHICLES: 2/site

OTHER: 6 people/site; 15-day stay limit

Wild Rice Camp in early September on Tubbs Lake. Participants learn how to make their own wooden tools for harvesting; how to collect, store, and prepare the rice; and how to reseed and restore wild-rice populations at other locations.

The two campgrounds on Tubbs Lake are part of Pere Marquette State Forest, and both are operated by Mecosta County Parks. Each campground offers sites on the water and easy boat access for getting out on the lake. The more interesting of the pair is the Tubbs Island Campground. Situated on a small island accessed by a narrow strip of land that passes through cattails, purple loosestrifes, and pickerelweed, this campground is wonderfully secluded. Across the way, campers will still see boats along the shore, cottages here and there, and the hard-to-ignore Tubbs Lake Resort (a private campground easily recognized by the rows of RVs and fifth-wheel trailers), but the island offers a sense of privacy that's much appreciated by campers.

Tubbs Island Campground has 12 sites, all but 2 of which are on the water. Sites 1–7 are on the high end of the island and overlook the lake. Sites 1–3 face the lake's more open water. Sites 8–10, near the low side, offer semiobstructed views of the water, which is blocked by trees and, in the case of 10, cattails and such.

Personally, I prefer the two walk-in sites, 11 and 12. Campers looking for a little more isolation will drive the one-way loop around the campground and find, just as the loop ends, a small area for parking on the left. From there, it's a short hike up the hill to one of the two sites. Though not right on the water, both sit high on the wooded hill, overlooking the lake.

The Martiny Chain of Lakes is fed by Chippewa Creek, which flows into Saddlebag Lake at the west end of the flooding. It exits over the Winchester Dam in the east as the Chippewa River, eventually flowing into the Tittabawassee, which empties into the Saginaw, which in turn empties into Saginaw Bay near Bay City. The eastern arm of Tubbs Lake stretches due east from Tubbs Island, around a final promontory—which is also where you'll find Tubbs Lake Mainland Campground. (The campgrounds are a little more than a mile apart by road: to reach Tubbs Lake Mainland from Tubbs Island, simply get back on Madison Road heading east; then turn left on Birch Haven Drive and follow the signs.)

Tubbs Mainland Campground is laid out like a strand of Christmas lights, with a small loop of six sites at the end. More than half of the campground's 21 sites look out over the

Tubbs Lake State Forest Campgrounds

water. Sites 1–9 are set back a little in the woods. Site 10 is half woods with some waterfront. During our last visit, I regretted not being able to pitch our tent on site 11 or 12—both were very picturesque.

Surrounded by 1,600 acres of the Martiny Lake State Game Area, a property full of woods and wetlands, the region is considered a sportsman's paradise by many regulars. The lakes are dotted with boat launches, and the game area encompasses more bodies of water than just those of the lake chain. Bluegill, Bass, Mud, and Half-Moon Lakes all abut at least a portion of this retreat for hunters and anglers. (Duck hunting is also popular here.)

Further downstream, closer to Mount Pleasant, the Chippewa River is popular with tubers, but paddlers jump in not far from here. Just about 7 miles northeast, a dam in Barryton collects the west and north branches of the river. Paddlers put in at the dam and enjoy more than 80 miles of picturesque canoeing. But there's really no need to go so far a-paddle to enjoy some time on the water. An entire day could be spent fishing or simply exploring the Martiny Lakes, and even more if you ventured into nearby Pretty Lake or Jehnsen Lake.

GETTING THERE

From the west: From Maple Street in Big Rapids, head south on Third Avenue and, in 0.2 mile, turn left (east) onto Colburn Avenue/16 Mile Road. In 8.3 miles, bear left (north) onto 110th Avenue; then, in 1 mile, turn right (east) onto 17 Mile Road. In 2 miles, turn right (south) onto 90th Avenue and, in 0.5 mile, turn left (east) onto Wilson Road. In 0.7 mile, curve right (south) as Wilson becomes 80th Avenue; then, in 1.2 miles, continue straight (east) on Taft Road. In 1.4 miles, turn left (north) onto 65th Avenue, which curves right and becomes Madison Road in 1.2 miles. In 0.2 mile, turn left (north) onto 65th Avenue to reach Tubbs Island Campground, about 0.4 mile ahead at the end of the road.

From the east: From Mission Street in Mount Pleasant, head west on M-20 and, in about 19 miles, turn right (north) onto M-66. After 8 miles, turn left (west) onto 17 Mile Road. In 1.5 miles, turn left (south) onto 45th Avenue; then, in 0.7 mile, turn right (west) onto Madison Road. In 1.2 miles, turn right (north) onto Birch Haven Drive and follow it 0.5 mile to the entrance for Tubbs Lake Mainland Campground, on your left.

GPS COORDINATES:

Tubbs Island Campground N43° 42.834' W85° 12.624'

Tubbs Mainland Campground N43° 42.449' W85° 11.901'

12

⚠ Warren Dunes State Park:
RUSTIC CAMPGROUND

Beauty ★★★★★ Privacy ★★★★ Spaciousness ★★★★★ Quiet ★★★★★ Security ★★★★★
Cleanliness ★★★★★

Warren Dunes is a nice campground with plenty of trails for hiking, dunes for climbing, and beaches for swimming.

The southwest corner of Michigan is the domain of Chicagoans. That may be overstating it a bit, but it's hard to understate the influence that Chicago has had on the development of tourism along this stretch of Lake Michigan shoreline. Dig a little into the history of many local restaurants and inns, and somewhere in their past you will likely find stories of some family from the Windy City who decided to move to southwest Michigan to make a go of it in the service industry. Of course, much of the coast has been built up on this side of the state, but folks from Illinois and Indiana, with just the weekend to recreate, find Harbor Country an easy drive.

In the midst of marinas, public beaches, summer homes, and burger joints, Warren Dunes State Park offers a surprisingly pleasant natural retreat. That is not to say that the park stands

An overcast sky softens the Lake Michigan shoreline at Warren Dunes.

Photo: Hank Erdmann/Shutterstock

KEY INFORMATION

CONTACT: Michigan DNR–Warren Dunes
State Park, 269-426-4013, michigan.gov
/warrendunes; reservations: 800-447-2757,
midnrreservations.com

OPEN: April–October

SITES: 37

EACH SITE HAS: Picnic table and fire pit

ASSIGNMENT: Online or by phone

REGISTRATION: At park office

AMENITIES: Well water and vault toilets

PARKING: At sites

NIGHTLY FEE: $25

ELEVATION: 651'

RESTRICTIONS

PETS: On leash only

FIRES: Fire pits only

ALCOHOL: Prohibited April–September

VEHICLES: Michigan Recreation Passport
required (see page 8); 2 vehicles/site

OTHER: 6 people/site; 15-day stay limit

as some bastion of solitude. With 3 miles of beach, a towering dune, and sand-side concessions and restrooms, the park can get downright crowded on sunny summer days. What often get overlooked are campgrounds. The park has two: one modern and one rustic.

Roads give visitors access only to the southern half of the park. The rustic campground lies along a loop at the northernmost end of the road. Campers can pitch their tents with the satisfaction of knowing that the milling crowds of sunbathers are more than 2 miles away in the day-use area. The rustic campground has 37 sites, which have fire pits and picnic tables and are serviced by four vault toilets and a well for water. Many of the sites, especially those along the eastern edge of the loop, are out in the open. Grassy and sunny, the ground is perfect for pitching a tent, though the sites offer little privacy. Even those in the woods along the other side of the loop have little undergrowth to screen the neighbors.

The best site of the bunch has to be site 1 (site 2 is a close runner-up). Because the campground is on a one-way loop, all sites experience the same amount of traffic. Right at the entrance, however, bushes and trees offer campers a feeling of solitude. I also think sites 24 and 26 are pretty nice, tucked into the trees as they are.

The modern campground, on the other hand, is much larger. It has 182 sites on two large loops, each divided by an extra row of campsites. There are modern restrooms with hot showers, playgrounds for the kids, and even a small general store. Even with all the hoopla, this campground would make a fine alternative if the rustic sites were booked or if your party includes campers who prefer to be a little closer to flush toilets. The sites offer more privacy between neighbors, and the ground is a combination of packed earth and gravel and grass.

The attraction of the beach is obvious, but this strip of sand is a bare fraction of the park's 1,952 acres. If you were to walk inland from Lake Michigan, up and over the foredunes and the backdunes, your path would trace the life cycle of a dune, from the active modern dunes by the lake to ancient dunes covered in a climax forest of beech and maple. The dips in between the parallel rows of hills contain unique biological ecosystems. In spring and early summer, you will find swaths of wildflowers; in the fall, the maples turn vibrant shades of orange and red.

Allowing visitors access to the more remote portions of the park, 6 miles of trails wind through Warren Dunes. You can find trailheads at the end of the beach parking lot and in both campgrounds. The dune environment, built on sand as it is, tends to be fragile; as such, the paths are designated for hiking and cross-country skiing—no horses and no mountain bikes.

The very existence of this natural preserve in the heart of Harbor Country is the result of one man's foresight. E. K. Warren, a businessman from Three Oaks, purchased the property in 1880. The land wasn't much use for farming, and locals considered the property so worthless that many allowed ownership to revert to the state in lieu of paying property tax. Needless to say, his purchase was considered foolish at best. In 1930, the dunes were established as a state park. (For another of Warren's preserves, check out Warren Woods State Park, 3 miles north of Three Oaks.)

The park has not been immune to a series of blights that have destroyed trees in recent years. In response to the emerald ash borer beetle, more than 4,000 trees were removed from the park. It's easy to imagine what impact this has had on the landscape, though first-time visitors may not notice the loss.

Still, it's a nice campground with plenty of trails for hiking, dunes for climbing, and beaches for swimming. All this, and a cheeseburger at Redamak's Tavern in New Buffalo is just a 10-minute drive away.

Warren Dunes State Park: Rustic Campground

GETTING THERE

From Exit 16 off I-94 in Bridgman, take Red Arrow Highway south. The park entrance is a little more than 2 miles ahead, on the right. Take the first right after entering the park and drive 0.8 mile to the campground entrance, on your left.

GPS COORDINATES: N41° 54.636' W86° 35.304'

13

⛺ Yankee Springs State Recreation Area:
DEEP LAKE RUSTIC CAMPGROUND

Beauty ★★★★★ Privacy ★★★★ Spaciousness ★★★★★ Quiet ★★★★ Security ★★★★★ Cleanliness ★★★★★

The trailhead for one of southwest Michigan's best mountain biking rides is found near the entrance of the campground.

Rustic campgrounds in Michigan tend to be low-key. Typically, the state forest service will plot a couple dozen sites near a lake or river, dig a pit or two for vault toilets, drill a hole for a hand-pumped well, and throw up a sign welcoming campers to XYZ Campground. It's a formula that works and has come to define a level of roughing it that is replicated all over the state. If a campground grows much larger than this, you start finding flush toilets and hot showers, and then it's not long before someone is paving sites for RVs and closing sites to build comfy minicabins for the tentless.

Yankee Springs Recreation Area bucks this trend. In addition to a hugely popular modern campground on Gun Lake, the park maintains what may be the largest rustic campground in the state. More than 3.5 miles away on the eastern edge of the park, Deep Lake Rustic Campground has 78 sites on four loops. Each loop is poised on the top of a bluff overlooking the water. The campground sits high, maybe 50 feet, above the lake, and no sites are along the shore; the drop is simply too steep. This unique configuration results in loops that are quite separate from each other. You may see the outline of a neighbor's tent through the woods, but between loops the land dips into small ravines.

The lower-numbered sites in the two northernmost loops tend to be paired together. Sites 17 and 18, for example, have their own picnic tables and fire pits, but they share the

Fall color festoons the forest adjacent to Deep Lake.

Photo: David Juckett

KEY INFORMATION

CONTACT: Michigan DNR–Yankee Springs State Recreation Area, 269-795-9081, michigan.gov/yankeesprings; reservations: 800-447-2757, midnrreservations.com

OPEN: April–November

SITES: 78

EACH SITE HAS: Picnic table and fire pit

ASSIGNMENT: Online or by phone

REGISTRATION: At park office, or self-register if office is closed

AMENITIES: Well water and pit toilets

PARKING: At sites

NIGHTLY FEE: $17

ELEVATION: 867'

RESTRICTIONS

PETS: On leash only

FIRES: Fire pits only

ALCOHOL: Prohibited

VEHICLES: Michigan Recreation Passport required (see page 8); 2 vehicles/site

OTHER: 6 people/site; 15-day stay limit

---

same clearing in the trees—offering virtually no privacy unless your party takes up both sites. Sites such as 38, 39, and 41 have a great view of the water, but none are right on it.

The two southernmost loops—sites 86–95 and 98–116—are smaller, more intimate, and deeper into the woods. In the distance, you can view the lake through the trees, but generally these sites are more private. On the side of the road, between clumps of campsites, sites 106 and 107 are particularly set apart—not on the water but with nice scenery nonetheless.

The trailhead for one of southwest Michigan's best mountain biking rides is found near the entrance of the campground. Thirteen miles of trails, ranging from easy to technical, take riders throughout the northeast portion of the recreation area. Along the way, the path passes Devil's Soupbowl (a glacially carved kettle formation), Graves Hill Overlook (just what it sounds like), and The Pines (an area of tall trees planted in the 1940s).

A sign at the trailhead for the bike path reads TRAILS PASS THROUGH OPEN HUNTING AREAS: WEAR BRIGHT COLORS. Heed this notice: hunting is popular here and in neighboring Barry State Game Area. This is the kind of advice that, if neglected, will suddenly come to mind when you're a mile into the woods and hear not-so-distant gunshots.

On laid-back summer weekends, Yankee Springs attracts big crowds. Thankfully for tent campers, most steer clear of Deep Lake, which doesn't have a beach. Gun Lake is the prime destination for sunbathing and swimming. Along Murphy's Point, which juts out into the lake just south of the modern campground, the park maintains three sandy beaches and a boat launch. The point's three large parking areas, bathhouses, picnic areas, and concessions give beachgoers everything they need for a day on the water.

Anglers will find access for fishing on most of the lakes in Yankee Springs, and these are all easy to get to from Gun Lake Road or Chief Noonday Road.

Those interested in Michigan's history—especially stories of its native peoples—will be interested to know about Chief Noonday (known alternatively as Nau-on-qual-que-zhick and Nau-qua-ga-sheek). In the early 19th century, he was chief of the Ottawa in a village that is now Grand Rapids. He later settled south of here in Prairieville, and the Yankee Springs area is known as a place where his people hunted game. History tells us that he fought on the side of the British in the War of 1812 and later signed treaties with the

American government, surrendering huge tracts of Ottawa land, thus opening up Ohio and Michigan for settlement.

Chief Noonday's legacy lives on. Grand Rapids recently unveiled a statue to commemorate his life, and his name is tacked on to local streets and, in the park, a lake, trail, and nature center. If traditional accounts can be trusted, he lived to be nearly 100 years old and died here in Barry County.

Yankee Springs State Recreation Area: Deep Lake Rustic Campground

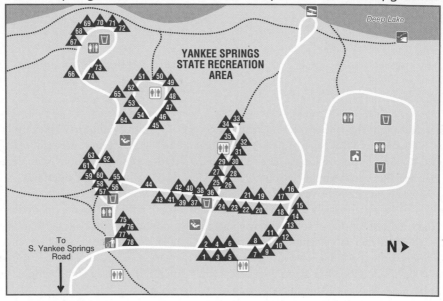

GETTING THERE

From US 131 near Shelbyville, take Exit 61 east onto 129th Avenue. In about 7.5 miles, turn right (south) onto Briggs Road, which becomes Gun Lake Road heading east. In 4 miles, turn left onto South Yankee Springs Road; the campground entrance is 0.5 mile ahead, on the left side of the road.

GPS COORDINATES: N42° 37.026' W85° 27.192'

NORTHWEST MICHIGAN

Big Sable Point Lighthouse, Ludington State Park (see Campground 19, page 69)

Photo: Doug Lemke/Shutterstock

14

Arbutus Lake No. 4 State Forest Campground

Beauty ★★★★ Privacy ★★★ Spaciousness ★★★★ Quiet ★★★ Security ★★★★ Cleanliness ★★★★★

Almost any day, you can park at the nearby visitor center, walk down to the river, and see people out for a stroll by the water or sitting in the shade by the banks, with fishing poles in hand.

Traverse City, also known as the Cherry Capital of the World, is at the center of northwest Michigan tourism. And why not? The town rests at the base of Grand Traverse Bay, one of the state's most prized settings. Dozens of hotels, motels, and resorts serve the thousands of visitors who travel to this region for vacation. They come to sit on the beach and play miniature golf. They come for the National Cherry Festival and the Traverse City Film Festival. They come to explore art galleries in nearby Elk Rapids or Suttons Bay. And they come to tour some of the best orchards and wineries in the world.

Often lost on the casual tourist, however, is the accessibility of nature in and around Traverse City. Few visitors would describe the town as urban in character—a state park is on the main drag, for Pete's sake—but somehow it's easy to miss the trees for the forest.

A few miles southeast of town, where the natural setting is harder to ignore, the state forest maintains the Arbutus Lake No. 4 State Forest Campground on Arbutus Lake. In actuality, five smaller lakes make up Arbutus Lake. All told, they stretch 2 miles from one end to the other, connected by narrow channels. The lakes are numbered, 1–5, south–north. Campers flock to Lake No. 4 throughout the summer, making it one of the state's most popular rustic campgrounds.

This small rustic campground has 25 sites. Campers here come because they love water and woods. The rules for boating on Arbutus Lake favor anglers. A no-wake ordinance on Lakes No. 1 and No. 5 keeps loud water sports to a minimum, and quiet hours are enforced

Many campsites sit atop a hill, and steps lead down to the quiet lake.

KEY INFORMATION

CONTACT: Michigan DNR–Keith J. Charters Traverse City State Park, 231-922-5270, tinyurl.com/arbutuslake. Canoes can be rented for 4- and 9-mile trips from Ranch Rudolf (231-947-9529, ranchrudolf.com), about 6 miles east of Arbutus Lake on Ranch Rudolf Road.

OPEN: Year-round, though snow may prevent access

SITES: 25

EACH SITE HAS: Picnic table and fire pit

ASSIGNMENT: First come, first served; no reservations. Arrive by midmorning and have a plan in place in case the campground is full.

REGISTRATION: Self-register at campground

AMENITIES: Hand-pumped potable water and pit toilets

PARKING: At sites

NIGHTLY FEE: $15

ELEVATION: 872'

RESTRICTIONS

PETS: On leash only

FIRES: Fire pits only

ALCOHOL: Permitted

VEHICLES: Michigan Recreation Passport required (see page 8); 2 vehicles/site

OTHER: 6 people/site; 15-day stay limit

on Nos. 2, 3, and 4. So from 10 at night until 6:30 the next morning, motorboats have to keep to a low speed, and water-skiing is prohibited. Tent campers see this as a boon, especially those who appreciate the sounds of nature when settling into a sleeping bag.

The hilly terrain is a remnant of the last glacial period. (As the final glaciers retreated, they left tons upon tons of stones and dirt, scraped up over the centuries of their slow advance.) Camp planners plotted these sites around a steep hill overlooking the north end of Lake No. 4, taking full advantage of the topography. Several of the sites closest to the lake sit above the road or below, requiring campers to park their vehicles alongside the road and take the stairs. Both options provide campsites that overlook the water and keep the road out of sight.

With 25 sites, the campground remains quiet even when full (that is, every weekend in the summer). A few years ago, the number of campsites had to be reduced due to budget concerns, but as a positive result, the campground is quieter than it used to be. Each site has a fire pit and a picnic table. Pit toilets maintain the rustic theme, and campers hand-pump water from the well.

While no readily accessible trails for hiking connect to the campground, the dirt roads in the area wind in and around a dozen or so smaller lakes. These would be fun to explore on a mountain bike. Arbutus Lake No. 5 Park, operated by East Bay Township, has a beach and nice shady picnic area. The lake itself attracts anglers looking for largemouth bass, and a boat ramp is available. The nearby Boardman River makes for a gentle canoe ride (see Key Information, above, for rental information).

An impressive abundance of wildlife thrives around Arbutus. Visitors often spot blue herons wading in the shallows, and the Michigan Department of Natural Resources designated the entire Arbutus Lake a loon habitat. More than a few bald eagles call the area home, though sightings are still rare enough to be breathtaking. Bald eagles have made a comeback in Michigan, especially in the north. The state now counts nearly 500, from fewer than 100 nests 40 years ago. In fact, authorities removed the birds from the state and federal endangered species lists in 2009.

Though it takes only 10 minutes to drive to Traverse City from the campground, a more ancient waterway connects the two points. The Boardman River flows from headwaters east of Kalkaska. On its way, a nest of lakes southeast of Traverse City indirectly feeds the river—the largest are Spider Lake, Rennie Lake, and Arbutus Lake. Here, pine trees paint the air with their rich scent. The river continues on.

Trace the river on a map and it flows through Brown Bridge (before it was drained), Keystone, and Sabin Ponds, and downstream to Boardman Lake. The Boardman River winds through the heart of town to where it empties into the bay. Behind Front Street, tall shady trees line the river. Almost any day, you can park at the nearby visitor center, walk down to the river, and see people out for a stroll by the water or sitting in the shade by the banks, with fishing poles in hand.

In fact, parks and nature preserves hang on the winding strand of the Boardman like beads on a necklace. Campers looking to stretch their legs and explore will find plenty of fun near the water, from quiet nature hikes to dining in town.

Arbutus Lake No. 4 State Forest Campground

GETTING THERE

From US 31 in Traverse City, drive 9.5 miles south on Garfield Avenue (which becomes Garfield Road), and turn left (east) on Potter Road (watch for the blinking caution light). Drive a little more than 4 miles to Four Mile Road, and turn right (south); then, in 0.5 mile, turn left (east) onto North Arbutus Lake Road. The park is a little less than a mile ahead, on the right side of the road.

Note: If you're trying another route, some maps of the area show Four Mile Road going all the way through to North Arbutus Lake Road from US 31—not true. It's best to stick with Garfield Road or, alternatively, Three Mile Road.

GPS COORDINATES: N44° 40.716' W85° 31.350'

15

CCC Bridge State Forest Campground

Beauty ★★★★ Privacy ★★★ Spaciousness ★★★★ Quiet ★★★ Security ★★★★ Cleanliness ★★★★★

Even if your plans don't include a canoe, kayak, or inner tube, a quiet spot along the Manistee River shouldn't be overlooked.

It's intriguing to realize how close the Au Sable and Manistee Rivers in northern Michigan are to each other on the map. Both originate just south of Gaylord, run a parallel path south, and suddenly part near Grayling—the Au Sable eventually finding Lake Huron; the Manistee, Lake Michigan. Lake Margrethe, west of Grayling, was once known as Portage Lake, a name that is still attached to its creek, which empties into the Manistee. On a good map, you can see why. Old-time travelers crossing Michigan's Lower Peninsula would have found the several-mile portage from the Au Sable to Lake Margrethe an easy alternative to paddling around the tip of the mitt. In fact, long-distance paddlers still tackle the 270-mile route today.

The Au Sable River is the more popular of the two in this part of the state, but I suspect that has more to do with easy accessibility in Grayling than a comparison of each river's qualities. The Upper Manistee is protected as part of the Michigan Natural Rivers Program, while the Lower Manistee has been designated a National Wild and Scenic River. All told, the river enjoys a fine reputation among paddlers and anglers, and you will regularly see hordes of kids floating by camp in tubes. Two canoe liveries, one in Grayling and another in Kalkaska (see next page), offer trips that cover most of this upper portion of the river.

The amenities here are basic, but recreational opportunities abound.

Photo: Kate Redding/thedyrt.com

KEY INFORMATION

CONTACT: Michigan DNR–Keith J. Charters Traverse City State Park, 231-922-5270, tinyurl.com/cccbridgecampground. Canoe liveries on the Manistee include Shel-Haven Canoe and Kayak Rental in Grayling (989-348-2158, shelhaven.com) and Long's Canoe Livery in Kalkaska (989-348-7224 or 231-258-3452, longscanoelivery.com).

OPEN: Year-round, though snow may prevent access

SITES: 31

EACH SITE HAS: Picnic table and fire pit

ASSIGNMENT: First come, first served; no reservations

REGISTRATION: Self-register at campground

AMENITIES: Hand-pumped water and vault toilets

PARKING: At sites

NIGHTLY FEE: $15

ELEVATION: 1,082'

RESTRICTIONS

PETS: On leash only

FIRES: Fire pits only

ALCOHOL: Permitted

VEHICLES: Michigan Recreation Passport required (see page 8); 2 vehicles/site

OTHER: 6 people/site; 15-day stay limit

The CCC Bridge is the perfect spot for a campground. Thru-paddlers, of course, appreciate any nice place to stop for the night. Day-trippers putting in near M-72 in Grayling will find, 5–7 hours later, the CCC Bridge waiting in the distance. A parking lot at the entrance to the South Campground serves paddlers and tubers, and vans arrive pretty regularly, especially on weekends, to pull groups from the water. But even if your plans don't include a canoe, kayak, or inner tube, a quiet spot along the Manistee River shouldn't be overlooked. Its humble scenic charms are worth a stay.

As the campground is designed for campers with tents and small trailers, bigger rigs tend to find other places to set up. The campground straddles the river at CCC Bridge. North of the bridge, a small outpost of seven sites lies along a single road with a turnaround at the end. Of these, site 4 is the only one not on the river. Separated by a road, a river, and the bridge, the North Campground is the quieter of the two. The sites here are grassy, and the river is seen easily through the trees.

The South Campground has the other 24 sites. Thirteen of them can be found on three loops that follow the contour of the water. The land behind the first loop (sites 9–13) seemed boggy on my last visit. Farther along, the second loop (sites 14–18) is on higher ground. A pathway from behind 17 and 18 leads down to the river. Views of the river here are harder to come by, even though the water is flowing just beyond the trees.

The remaining sites lie along a spur to the south of camp. Nestled in pinewoods, the sites here are lined with packed dirt and the reddish hue of pine needles. These sites are the farthest from the water, and, during the height of mosquito season, this might offer some respite from the buzzing horde.

Upstream from CCC Bridge, the state maintains three campgrounds—Lake Margrethe (just south of where the lake flows into Portage Creek), Manistee River Bridge (near M-72), and Upper Manistee River. Like CCC Bridge, they all offer rustic amenities: water from a hand pump and vault toilets.

You can find the headwaters of the Manistee north of the Upper Manistee Campground near the ghost town of Deward in the 4,700-acre Deward Tract, which is part of the Au Sable

State Forest. The tract features the state's only Pine Stump Preserve—42.5 acres that have been set aside to "protect the evidence of early logging efforts in Michigan" (as described by the Michigan Department of Natural Resources).

The water between M-72 and CCC Bridge is prime fly-fishing water. In fact, that's the only fishing allowed here. The warm-water fishery at Lake Margrethe supports a fine population of smallmouth bass and muskies, but the cold Manistee is all about the trout. Anglers will tell you that this river produces some of the largest trout you will ever catch on a fly.

CCC Bridge State Forest Campground

GETTING THERE

From the Y-intersection of McClellan Street, M-72 West, and M-72 East in Grayling, take M-72 West, which is also M-93 South. About 1.4 miles out of town, the road forks—where M-72 heads right, bear left (south) onto M-93; then, in 2.2 miles, bear right around the traffic circle to continue south and west on Howe Road, which later becomes Military Road SE. In about 14 miles, turn right (north) onto Sunset Trail Road SE; the campground is 1.8 miles ahead, on the north and south sides of the road and river.

GPS COORDINATES:
North Campground N44° 36.919' W84° 59.542'
South Campground N44° 36.846' W84° 59.436'

16

Fisherman's Island State Park Campgrounds

Beauty ★★★★★ Privacy ★★★★ Spaciousness ★★★★ Quiet ★★★★★ Security ★★★★ Cleanliness ★★★★★

This park is truly one of the region's treasures. Yet if it weren't for the small brown signs on US 31, you would miss it altogether.

From Traverse City and points south, US 31 parallels the shore of Grand Traverse Bay, about a mile inland. The road essentially shoots straight north from Eastport until you get to the curve into Charlevoix, but the drive is anything but boring. Gently rolling hills make it possible to catch glimpses of Grand Traverse Bay to the west, and orchards, farm markets, and a couple of art galleries line the way. As you approach Charlevoix, the terrain levels out and the road bends to the northeast. Here, between US 31 and Lake Michigan, lies Fisherman's Island State Park.

West of the main road, you find forests of maples, birches, and aspens, as well as cedar bogs and stands of black spruce. Nearly 2,700 acres of secluded forest sit on 6 miles of Lake Michigan shoreline, all surprisingly close to one of the busiest tourist towns in northwestern Michigan. And tucked into this rugged paradise, two surprisingly low-key campgrounds wait on Lake Michigan. The park is truly one of the region's treasures. Yet if it weren't for the small brown signs on US 31, you would miss it altogether.

A brilliant sunset graces Fisherman's Island State Park.

KEY INFORMATION

CONTACT: Michigan DNR–Fisherman's Island State Park, 231-547-6641, michigan.gov /fishermansisland; reservations: 800-447-2757, midnrreservations.com

OPEN: May–late September

SITES: 80

EACH SITE HAS: Picnic table and fire pit

ASSIGNMENT: Online or by phone

REGISTRATION: With campground host at site 1

AMENITIES: Water and pit toilets

PARKING: At sites

NIGHTLY FEE: $17

ELEVATION: 642'

RESTRICTIONS

PETS: On leash only

FIRES: Fire pits only

ALCOHOL: Permitted

VEHICLES: Michigan Recreation Passport required (see page 8); 2 vehicles/site

OTHER: 6 people/site; 15-day stay limit

Much of the history you hear about this stretch of Lake Michigan, between Grand Traverse and Little Traverse Bays, centers on Michigan's lumber heyday. Lumber towns quickly sprang to life along the shore, only to sink back into the wilderness when the lumbermen had cut all they could find and moved on. The long docks of Antrim—immortalized in Nancy Stone's children's novel *Whistle Up the Bay*—used to stretch out into the steel-blue water, just a few miles south of the park. Today, all that is left of Antrim are a cemetery and rumors of submerged posts in the water.

Loggers, however, were not the area's first residents: the Ottawa were living here when Europeans arrived. Earlier still, the Archaic people passed through this way, and archaeologists have found evidence that as far back as 6,000 years ago, Woodland American Indians would come here in the summer months to mine the local chert for material to make tools.

Archaeologists left the excavation sites unmarked, but few people come to Fisherman's Island for a history lesson. They come for the woods, the beach, and the excellent camping. A stretch of private shoreline divides the park into two sections. The northern portion has the campgrounds, marked trails, and picnic areas.

The main road through the north end of the park begins at Bells Bay Road, parallels the shore of Lake Michigan for 2.5 miles, and ends in a gravel parking lot at Inwood Creek, where you'll find a shady picnic area and a narrow footbridge. Beyond the bridge, a trail continues a couple of thousand feet out to a sandy point. The beach can be accessed from anywhere along the path. From here, you can see the island from which the park gets its name.

Loops off the main road define the park's North Campground and South Campground. The North Campground (sites 1–35) has two loops, but campers best appreciate it for a row of sought-after lakeside sites. These campsites (9 and 26–35) are nestled in a band of cedar and birch trees, right on the lake. Just yards from the shore of Lake Michigan, they fill up fast in the summer. The reservation system doesn't allow you to request specific sites; you can, however, note your preference, and they will accommodate you if a site is available.

The first loop, sites 2–8, is open only to tent camping (site 1 is reserved for the campground host). The sites here have plenty of room to spread out, but there's not much privacy. The second loop of this campground and the South Campground loop, 1.5 miles farther, make good use of the woods. Even campers sited across the road from each other will appreciate a sense of seclusion. The topography gets interesting as you move inland, and the sites on these loops use the steep terrain creatively.

Fisherman's Island Foot Trail, which begins near the park entrance and ends at the parking area at Inwood Creek, offers a pleasant hike that will get you back into the woods. Along the way it follows the ridges behind the two campgrounds. Several trails connect the main path with both campgrounds and the main road. Cross-country skiers and snowshoers use the trail in the winter.

For a more remote adventure, drive south to the southern part of the park. You get there from the village of Norwood. Lake Street, as it is called in town, is a rutted doubletrack that winds 2.3 miles north to Whiskey Creek. Only the most rugged vehicles will make the entire trip. Others will drop to the wayside and their passengers will have to hike the rest of the way.

This section of the park has no amenities—no picnic tables, toilets, or water. As such, visitors have to pack in everything they need. The payoff, however, is nearly 3 miles of unspoiled Lake Michigan beach and access to the remotest parts of the park's sprawling acreage.

Fisherman's Island State Forest Campground

GETTING THERE

From the intersection of US 31 and M-66 in Charlevoix, head west on US 31. In 1.3 miles, turn right onto Bells Bay Road, and take it 1.6 miles west and then north to the park entrance. The North Campground is 0.2 mile ahead on your left; the South Campground is 1.5 miles farther, also on your left.

GPS COORDINATES:
  North Campground N45° 18.310' W85° 18.800'
  South Campground N45° 17.598' W85° 19.994'

17

⛺ Graves Crossing State Forest Campground

Beauty ★★★★★ Privacy ★★★★ Spaciousness ★★★★★ Quiet ★★★★ Security ★★★★ Cleanliness ★★★★

The Jordan River was the first waterway in Michigan to be designated as a National Wild and Scenic River.

The big territorial surveys of years ago sought to impose some order upon Michigan's wild landscape. In most cases, county and township boundaries line up true—north and south, east and west. County roads follow the same bearings, divvying up the state into manageable grids. We tend to take this superimposed order for granted. It's only when you pay attention to nature that you see things differently. Oddly placed villages and roads that don't line up take on new significance. First, you notice that most towns, for example, are near a lake or river—the bigger the city, the more significant the nearby waterway. When you see the words *portage* or *traverse* on a map, the history of the place suddenly comes to life.

Today, when people only walk cross-country or travel by canoe for recreation, the logic of the old pathways seems part of the dim past. M-66 is a road that defies the usual logic. It sort of staggers north by northwest from Mancelona to East Jordan—getting where it needs

Canoeists and kayakers flock to this tranquil campground.

KEY INFORMATION

CONTACT: Michigan DNR–Young State Park, 231-582-7523, tinyurl.com/gravescrossing. Canoes can be rented on Graves Crossing Road at Swiss Hideaway Canoe Rental (231-536-2341, jordanriverfun.com).

OPEN: Year-round, though snow may prevent access

SITES: 10

EACH SITE HAS: Picnic table and fire pit

ASSIGNMENT: First come, first served; no reservations

REGISTRATION: Self-register at campground

AMENITIES: Hand-pumped potable water and pit toilets

PARKING: At sites

NIGHTLY FEE: $15

ELEVATION: 658'

RESTRICTIONS

PETS: On leash only

FIRES: Fire pits only

ALCOHOL: Permitted

VEHICLES: Michigan Recreation Passport required (see page 8); 2 vehicles/site

OTHER: 6 people/site; 15-day stay limit

to go but always defying a straight line. Stop anywhere along this road and hoof it east into the woods, and you'll see why: the road is following the curves of the Jordan River. The river springs up from its headwaters northeast of Mancelona and winds south and then north again toward Lake Charlevoix. The lush Jordan River Valley is thick with forest and is a popular destination for fall-color tourists. With steep hills on either side, the upper portion of the river flows through a valley nearly a mile wide.

About 9 miles north of Mancelona, Mackinaw State Forest keeps a campground at Graves Crossing. Two loops of five sites each make up the camp. The ground is flat, and the sites are floored with a mix of packed dirt and grass. The woods along this stretch of the river mainly feature pines and cedars, but you will also find the odd maple. Though the river lies just off sites 3, 7, and 8, it keeps its distance. You can hear the river nearby but can only see it through the undergrowth here and there. Both loops share a set of pit toilets and water from a hand pump.

M-66 runs right along one side of the campground. The road is hardly a busy thoroughfare, and there is a wide buffer of trees, but what traffic there is can be heard somewhat in camp. With no host on duty and a short walk from the main road, security is a question. However, as difficult as it is to find the narrow dirt drive into the campground during the day, I would tend not to worry about troublemakers stumbling in at night.

The Jordan was the first waterway in Michigan to be designated a National Wild and Scenic River. And that it is. The valley here was once logged clean—the lumber was sent down the river to mills in Boyne City and East Jordan. When farmers gave up trying to eke a living out of the poor soil, the state took back much of the land and let it go wild. While it's hard to imagine the ancient forest that was here more than a century ago, the new growth is impressive, especially in the fall when the view from Dead Man's Hill reveals miles upon miles of gold, red, and burnt orange.

Exploring the upper portions of the river means hiking the Jordan Valley Pathway. The lower portion, however, is best explored from the seat of a canoe. Just down the road from Graves Crossing, Swiss Hideaway Canoe Rental rents boats and puts people in the water (see Key Information for phone number). The place can get busy on the weekends. But even with other liveries bringing in groups, the Jordan is hardly an overpaddled river. From the campground to the takeout at Lake Charlevoix is a scenic 3- to 4-hour float.

For the rest of the river, you will find the main trailhead and parking area for the Jordan River Pathway due east of the campground off US 131 on Dead Man's Hill Road. The quickest way to the trailhead by car takes you 4.2 miles south on M-66 to Alba Road (County Road 620) and then east on Alba Road 4.3 miles to US 131 (also known as Mackinaw Trail). Six miles north you turn left on Dead Man's Hill Road. The trailhead is just 1.7 miles in. The trail closely follows the river all the way back to the Pinney Bridge Campground (Pinney Bridge Road is about 1.5 miles south of Graves Crossing). The trail crosses the road here, but there's no parking area. Access to the campground is limited to those who paddle or hike in. The trail then makes a wide loop south and then north again, crossing many of the creeks that feed the Jordan. It draws close to the river one last time before returning to the trailhead. The entire trip is 18 miles, and many people hike it with backpacks, spending the night at Pinney Bridge.

Graves Crossing State Forest Campground

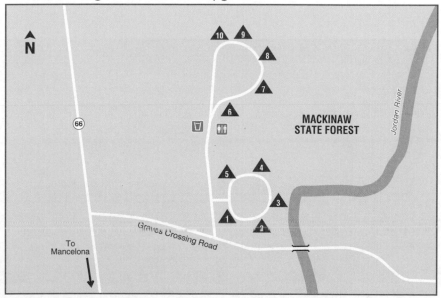

GETTING THERE

From State Street in Mancelona, head north on US 131 for 0.8 mile; then bear left at the fork onto M-66. Continue north on M-66 for 8.7 miles; then turn right onto Graves Crossing Road. The campground is on the left before the bridge.

GPS COORDINATES: N45° 02.016' W85° 03.918'

18

⚑ Lake Dubonnet State Forest Campground

Beauty ★★★★ Privacy ★★★★★ Spaciousness ★★★★★ Quiet ★★★★★ Security ★★★★★ Cleanliness ★★★★

The campground has 50 rustic sites on five loops nestled in a forest of tall pine along the shore of Lake Dubonnet.

US 31 shoots northward along the west side of the state, connecting cities along Lake Michigan from Holland and Grand Haven to Pentwater and Manistee. Then, after clipping the edge of Crystal Lake in Benzie County, the road makes a turn east, heading north again only when it is in line with Traverse City. (This leaves M-22 to skirt the shore around the Leelanau Peninsula.) So for about 20 miles, US 31 runs west–east, with Honor at one end and Chum's Corner at the other. Just east of the middle is Interlochen.

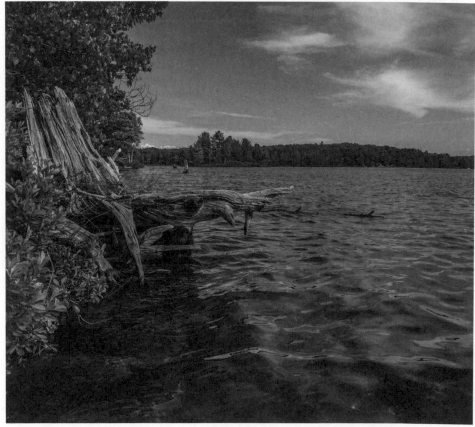

Island view on Lake Dubonnet

KEY INFORMATION

CONTACT: Interlochen State Park, 231-276-9511, tinyurl.com/lakedubonnet

OPEN: Year-round

SITES: 50

EACH SITE HAS: Picnic table and fire pit

ASSIGNMENT: First come, first served; no reservations

REGISTRATION: At self-register kiosk

AMENITIES: Hand-pumped potable water and pit toilets

PARKING: At sites

NIGHTLY FEE: $15

ELEVATION: 860'

RESTRICTIONS

PETS: On leash only

FIRES: In fire pits only

ALCOHOL: Permitted in campground only

VEHICLES: Michigan Recreation Passport required (see page 8); 2 vehicles/site

OTHER: 6 people/site; 14-day stay limit

Lake Dubonnet State Forest Campground sits on Lake Dubonnet in Grand Traverse County, less than 2 miles north of US 31. The campground has 50 rustic sites on five loops nestled in a forest of tall pine along the shore of Lake Dubonnet. Each site has a picnic table and fire ring. There are pit toilets, and water is available from hand pumps. At one end of the campground, there is a boat launch and parking area for day users. The lake is popular for pan fishing.

Because the sites are divided into smaller groups, the campground has excellent privacy. None of the sites are actually on the water, but those located at the north end of the campground are closer to the water and tend to be more popular. One loop, No. 5, is entirely inland, and the sites here are usually the last taken.

Campers can't make reservations in advance—sites are doled out on a first-to-arrive-gets-the-site basis. Thankfully, it's rare that the campground fills completely, and there's honestly not a bad site in the place.

Part of Traverse City State Forest, the campground is maintained by Interlochen State Park, just 5 miles away. The town of Interlochen is even closer than that, just east on US 31. Interlochen is famous for its art camp, and the state park is a great place for camping. The town is also where you will find gas and groceries and whatever other supplies you might need.

Two miles northwest of Lake Dubonnet is Lake Ann. Close as it is, it would be a shame to miss out on Lake Ann's nature trails. There are nearly 6 miles of multiuse trails at the west end of the lake. The woods here consist mostly of maple and beech. Popular in the winter with cross-country skiers, the Lake Ann Pathway features four scenic loops. Depending on the route taken, hikers can catch views of Lake Ann, Shavenaugh Lake, Mary's Lake, and Tarnwood Lake. The trails are also used by mountain bikers. Lake Ann features a smaller state forest campground as well.

Lake Dubonnet State Forest Campground

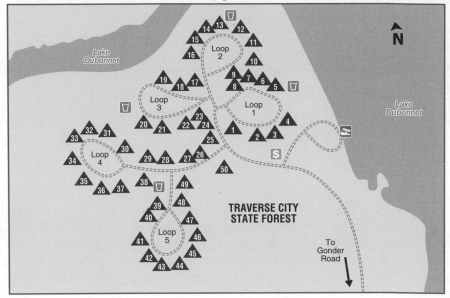

GETTING THERE

From US 31 just west of Interlochen, head north on Gonder Road, which becomes Camp Ground Road 1 mile farther at the intersection with Mud Lake Road. In another 0.7 mile, just past a boat launch and parking on the right, the road branches off into five campground loops.

GPS COORDINATES: N44° 40.399' W85° 47.884'

19

⛺ Ludington State Park:
JACK PINE WALK-IN CAMPGROUND

Beauty ★★★★★ Privacy ★★★★★ Spaciousness ★★★★★ Quiet ★★★★★ Security ★★★★
Cleanliness ★★★★★

This campground rewards you with quiet nights, when all you hear is the sound of waves on Lake Michigan.

Ask Michiganders their favorite place to camp, and you're likely to hear Ludington State Park more often than not. It's hard to overestimate the popularity of this 5,300-acre recreation destination nestled between Hamlin Lake and Lake Michigan. The park consistently earns top spots on the annual lists of Michigan's most popular attractions, best beaches, and favorite campgrounds.

Most visitors park alongside the drive up into the park, hoof it over the foredune, and then lay out their towels, coolers, and umbrellas on one of the most beautiful stretches of Lake Michigan beach. Others venture farther in. The river that empties Hamlin Lake into Lake Michigan sees a regular parade of inner-tubers floating from one lake to the other, then walking back through the park to put in on this side of the Hamlin Dam. The more adventurous try hiking and perhaps take the back trails to the Big Sable Point Lighthouse.

The park has three modern campgrounds: Pines, Cedars, and Beechwood. Among campgrounds packed with RVs, fifth-wheel trailers, pop-ups, and the occasional tent mansions, these aren't bad at all. The campgrounds conform to the interesting contours of the land, and this creates space for unique sites. Several years back, you would have found my tent pitched somewhere in the Beechwood Campground, perhaps at site 232 between the first two loops. There are a few choice sites like this one, somewhat set apart and close to Lost Lake.

A wooden dock overlooks a gorgeous lake in the wilderness.

Photo: ehrlif/Shutterstock

KEY INFORMATION

CONTACT: Michigan DNR–Ludington State Park, 231-843-2423, michigan.gov/ludington; reservations: 800-447-2757, midnrreservations.com

OPEN: Year-round

SITES: 10

EACH SITE HAS: Picnic table and fire pit

ASSIGNMENT: Online or by phone

REGISTRATION: At the campground building on M-116 as you drive into the park

AMENITIES: Hand-pumped water and pit toilets

PARKING: Lot near park entrance

NIGHTLY FEE: $20 ($17 off-season)

ELEVATION: 590'

RESTRICTIONS

PETS: On leash only and away from the water

FIRES: Fire pits only

ALCOHOL: Permitted

VEHICLES: Michigan Recreation Passport required (see page 8); 2 vehicles/site

OTHER: 6 people/site; 15-day stay limit

Today, however, you would find me hauling my gear on my back to the Jack Pine Walk-In Campground. Ten sites on two spurs are hunkered down in the sand behind the park's long foredune. To get there, campers have to follow Lighthouse Trail (essentially a sidewalk) a mile up the beach from the Pines Campground. You're free to use wagons, bikes, or even a wheelbarrow, if that's what you need, but vehicles are prohibited.

With the exception of jack pines and some juniper bushes, there is little vegetation, just dune grass and some frost grapevines. The first spur, with sites A–E, is more out in the open. Buried in a cluster of stunted pine trees, site E is the exception. It sits across the way from the other four sites and offers a private retreat, somewhat protected from the sun and wind. More shade can be found at site F on the campground's other spur. Bushes and low trees screen the remaining sites, G–J, from each other, but not so much from the sun.

This campground requires some extra work on the part of visitors. The park defines quiet hours at Jack Pine as "all the time" but "especially between 11 p.m. and 8 a.m.," and campers have to bag out their own trash and leave it in Dumpsters near the park entrance. The campground repays the attention with quiet nights, when all you hear is the sound of waves on Lake Michigan.

From the walk-in campground, you are already halfway to Big Sable Point Lighthouse, via Lighthouse Trail. This is the sister light to the Little Sable Lighthouse in Silver Lake, about 35 miles south of here. Built back in 1867, the tower was originally constructed of yellow brick. A few decades later, the brick began to crumble, and the lighthouse was reinforced with iron bands and concrete wrapped around its exterior. The work on the light required it to be painted. The black-and-white stripes you see today were chosen to make the lighthouse more visible during the day. For a small donation, visitors can climb the tower, but if you really want to experience life in a lighthouse, ask about the volunteer keeper program.

The lighthouse served many years guiding ships around the Grande Pointe au Sable but was apparently too little help for the *George F. Foster*, a schooner bound for Chicago with a load of lumber. The ship was blown ashore by a gale in the fall of 1872. You can explore the wreck, for what it is, without even getting your feet wet. The ship is right up on shore, not too far south of the Jack Pine Walk-In Campground. It's almost entirely buried by beach sand, but the park has thoughtfully marked off the ship's dimensions and posted an informative sign.

The hike out to the lighthouse is an easy, level, 2-mile walk from the main parking lot via the beach or the aforementioned Lighthouse Trail. A more roundabout path takes you into the heart of the park along the Lighthouse Trail. All told, Ludington State Park has 21.5 miles of trails offering a variety of experiences. To escape the beach, try hiking out along the Island Trail, which begins by traversing the chain of small islands that define Lost Lake and then follows the western edge of Hamlin Lake. Return via the Ridge and Lost Lake trails. For a short hike, head over to the visitor center. The Skyline Trail there climbs to the top of the dunes and follows a boardwalk along the high ridge.

For something altogether unique, Ludington State Park has a defined canoe trail. Boats can be rented there at the park, or you can bring your own. With paddle in hand, you put in at the boat launch near Hamlin Dam and follow the shoreline south. Several coves and channels keep the route interesting. Most of the park that you see from the water here is inaccessible to cars and foot traffic.

Ludington State Park: Jack Pine Walk-In Campground

GETTING THERE

In Ludington, follow US 10/Ludington Avenue westbound until it dead-ends, and turn right (north) onto North Lakeshore Drive. In about 2.5 miles, bear left at the fork onto M-116; the park is 4 miles ahead at the end of the road.

GPS COORDINATES: N44° 02.664' W86° 30.684'

20

⛺Nordhouse Dunes Wilderness Area:
DISPERSED CAMPGROUND

Beauty ★★★★★ Privacy ★★★★★ Spaciousness ★★★★★ Quiet ★★★★★ Security ★★★★★
Cleanliness ★★★★★

This wilderness area offers campers the opportunity to pitch a tent outside the confines of a formal campground.

In 1987 Congress passed the Michigan Wilderness Act, which identified regions within Michigan's national forests that were worthy of being restored to a natural state. The law created 10 wilderness areas that have changed the state's landscape, so to speak, for those who appreciate an unspoiled experience of nature. Today, more than 30 years later, not everyone has heard of the Horseshoe Bay Wilderness or the Big Island Lake Wilderness, but it's hard to imagine a Michigan without the Upper Peninsula's Sylvania Wilderness Area or the Lower Peninsula's Nordhouse Dunes.

Nordhouse Dunes Wilderness Area is the only such wild place in the Lower Peninsula. Composed of 3,450 acres, the park shares a border with Ludington State Park to the south and with Huron–Manistee National Forest to the north and east. The preserve's fourth boundary is 4 miles of undeveloped Lake Michigan shoreline. This wilderness area offers campers the opportunity to hike and explore the coastal dune regions of Lake Michigan, as

The setting sun softly lights a sculptural driftwood pile at Nordhouse Dunes.

KEY INFORMATION

CONTACT: Huron–Manistee National Forest, Cadillac/Manistee Ranger District; 231-723-2211, tinyurl.com/nordhouse duneswilderness

OPEN: Year-round but unmaintained in winter

SITES: NA

EACH SITE HAS: NA

ASSIGNMENT: First come, first served; no reservations

REGISTRATION: Self-register at campground

AMENITIES: Vault toilets at trailheads

PARKING: At trailhead parking areas

NIGHTLY FEE: None for camping; $5/day or $15/week vehicle fee for parking at trailhead

ELEVATION: 653'

RESTRICTIONS

PETS: On leash only

FIRES: Prohibited on beaches, as is collecting woody material from beaches or sandy areas

ALCOHOL: No stated restrictions; check ahead to confirm

VEHICLES: All motorized vehicles prohibited

OTHER: Campsites should be at least 400' from Lake Michigan, 250' from trails and Nordhouse Lake, and 450' from developed recreation area

well as to pitch a tent outside the confines of a formal campground (the U.S. Forest Service calls it dispersed camping).

I would recommend getting a good trail guide before diving into the Nordhouse Dunes. *Backpacking in Michigan* by Jim DuFresne is an excellent resource and describes 50 excellent places to backpack in the state, including the Nordhouse Dunes. For the purpose of this book, I will simply offer a bare sketch of one of many possible itineraries.

There are two main trailheads into the dunes. From the north, campers access the trails from Lake Michigan Recreation Area. From the south, there's a parking area and trailhead at the end of Nurnberg Road. Near the northern trailhead, a 122-step climb takes you to the top of an observation tower with breathtaking views of Lake Michigan. (Well, I'm sure the climb contributes a little to the lack of breath, but the view from up top is nevertheless outstanding.) The wilderness trails here no longer have names, but those familiar with the dunes might remember the route that was once known as the Michigan Trail. From the north, the old Michigan Trail runs south, parallel to the shore, for about 2 miles. The route features a nice walk over ancient dunes, straddling the line between forest and open sand. Eventually, the path leads inland and takes you to the southern trailhead, where you can find a path back to the recreation area to complete a 6-mile loop.

Dunes are forever evolving. Not only does the wind constantly shape the contours of the sand closest to the lake, but farther inland, where the older portions of the dunes lie, you can also find nature transforming the shifting sands to stable forest. From sandy hills to woods stocked with beeches, sugar maples, red and white oaks, and such evergreens as red and white pines, Nordhouse Dunes is a hands-on lesson in ecology.

The rules for camping in the dunes are fairly simple. You must camp more than 400 feet from the Lake Michigan shoreline, 250 feet from established trails and Nordhouse Lake, and 450 feet from the recreation area. You are asked not to camp in areas where signs indicate that it is prohibited, and one rule states that visitors shall not be naked in public. Aside from that, camp where you will and how you will. I would suggest, however, that setting up on the open dunes will lead to more sand in your tent, hair, and clothes than you can imagine. I prefer to seek the shelter of some trees.

Most campers will approach the dunes from US 31, making the final drive in on West Forest Trail Road or Nurnberg Road. The former, as the name suggests, leads to the day-use area and developed campground at Lake Michigan Recreation Area; the latter leads to the southern parking area and trailhead. Connecting the two, Green Road parallels, but sits just outside, the wilderness's eastern boundary. Along this narrow, sandy U.S. Forest Service road, three unofficial primitive sites offer visitors a convenient and rather secluded escape. The sites are bare-bones—no picnic tables, no sources of drinkable water, and no outhouses. A few have rudimentary pit toilets of the open-air-throne variety, but the nearest proper vault toilet is at the trailhead on Nurnberg Road.

Green Road is rough, but people find it possible to get small trailers onto these sites. With just three campsites spread out over a mile or so, there's plenty of room to spread out and lots of privacy. Typical of the dunes ecology, the sites are sandy, with dune grass growing in patches. Beeches and some evergreens provide shade, and, where the terrain falls away into lower land behind the campsites, the ground is blanketed in ferns.

For more-traditional car camping, consider a stay at **Lake Michigan Recreation Area Campground.** This national forest campground offers 99 sites on four loops, flush toilets, and direct trail access to the wilderness. The day-use area has a popular beach on Lake Michigan, bike trails, a playground, and a few nice hiking loops. This campground fills up in the summer, especially on weekends, so consider reservations (877-444-6777, recreation.gov/camping/campgrounds/233714). Only some sites can be reserved; the rest are yours on a first-come, first-served basis.

The wilderness area is home to wildlife including this eastern hogback snake.

Nordhouse Dunes Wilderness Area: Dispersed Campground

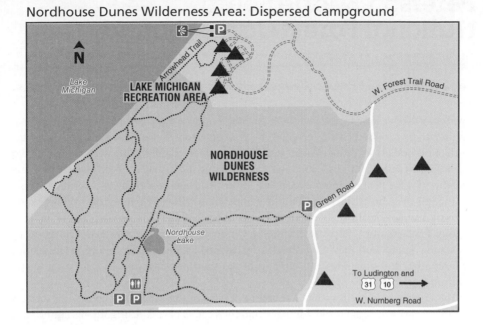

GETTING THERE

The wilderness area is located between Manistee and Ludington, west of US 31. From I-55 in Manistee, take US 31 South for 7.2 miles, and turn right (west) onto West County Line Road. In 1.2 miles, turn left (south) onto Quarterline Road; then, in 3.2 miles, turn right (west) onto West Forest Trail Road. In 5 miles, turn left to continue west on Forest Trail Road, and follow it 1.5 miles farther until it dead-ends at the day-use parking lot for Lake Michigan Recreation Area.

From US 10 east of Ludington, take US 31 North for 12 miles, and turn left (west) onto West Forest Trail Road. Drive 2.5 miles and turn left (south) onto Quarterline Road; then, in 4 miles, turn right (west) onto West Nurnberg Road, and proceed 6.3 miles to the dirt parking area for the Nurnberg Trailhead.

GPS COORDINATES:
Lake Michigan Recreation Area N44° 07.163' W86° 25.584'
Nurnberg Trailhead N44° 05.247' W86° 26.674'

21

⚠ Peterson Bridge South National Forest Campground

Beauty ★★★★★ Privacy ★★★★ Spaciousness ★★★★★ Quiet ★★★★ Security ★★★★★ Cleanliness ★★★★★

The riverfront sites at Peterson Bridge South are this wooded campground's hidden gems.

If you have taken canoe trips down the Pine River in the past, especially one organized by an outfitter, there is a good chance you have been to Peterson Bridge. There is a popular put-in north of the bridge for groups of paddlers. There are several large outfitters nearby (Pine River Paddlesports Center, Horina's Canoe and Kayak Rental, and just up the road a piece, Bosman's Pine River Canoe Rental), and they regularly drop off adventurers ready to tackle the river.

The put-in is directly across from the campground. The camp manager told me on my last visit that it's actually quite entertaining to sit on the bluff overlooking the put-in when a group first sets out. There are always a few people who have never been on the water in a canoe before, and inevitably they get all turned around trying to find their balance. At least a handful of canoes will flip and dump their passengers before they get even a hundred feet down the river.

The campground itself is a bit of a surprise. Drive through and you'll count only 20 sites. Because this is a national forest campground, the road is paved. A brightly lit bathroom in the center of the campground has drinking fountains, sinks, and flush toilets. There are additional vault toilets distributed throughout the camp. If this were all there was to Peterson

This large landing area sits just before a sharp bend in the river that takes paddlers underneath Peterson Bridge.

Photo: U.S. Forest Service (public domain)

KEY INFORMATION

CONTACT: Huron–Manistee National Forest, Baldwin/White Cloud Ranger District, 231-745-4631, tinyurl.com/petersonbridge

OPEN: Year-round, maintained May–October

SITES: 31

EACH SITE HAS: Picnic table, fire pit, lantern post

ASSIGNMENT: First come, first served; no reservations

REGISTRATION: Self-register at campground

AMENITIES: Vault toilets, modern restroom (no showers), drinking water

PARKING: At sites (or near entrance for walk-in sites)

NIGHTLY FEE: $21 ($7/person for walk-in sites)

ELEVATION: 838'

RESTRICTIONS

PETS: On leash only

FIRES: Fire pits only

ALCOHOL: No stated restrictions; check ahead to confirm

VEHICLES: 2/site

OTHER: 8 people/site; 14-day stay limit

Bridge, it would be a fine campground, but there's so much more. After leaving your car at the parking area near the registration kiosk, you'll take a path leading down to the river. This is the route to the campground's 11 walk-in/paddle-in campsites.

The first campsite as you walk is located on a rise overlooking the water. From this vantage point, campers can look across and down at the public put-in on the other side of the water. Continuing alongside the river, heading upstream, the path enters a quiet pocket of woods—northern cedars, oak, and maple, mostly. The forest floor is covered in ferns, and two campsites are set here against the bottom of the bluff.

Leaving the woods, the path ends at a sandy beach on the Pine River. This is where paddlers exit the river if they need a campsite for the night. For their convenience, there is a self-registration kiosk here, as well as drinking water. On either side of the sandy boat area are two campsites. Six more sit farther back—though the river bends around and two of these sites are close to the water.

The brush around these sites is full of poison ivy, so I wouldn't recommend tramping through the weeds. But the sites themselves are plenty spacious and well trimmed, so there's no real chance of accidentally stumbling into the noxious plant.

The river is so close here that you can hear it flowing as you drift off to sleep at night. Some say that flowing water creates negative ions, and negative ions are believed to help increase levels of serotonin in the body, helping to relieve stress and boost energy. If this is true and the science plays out, there's all the more reason to haul all that gear down to the river for some camping.

From these riverfront campsites, a stairway leads up the hill to the main campground. Halfway up you will pass a set of vault toilets, but continue to the top, and the modern restrooms are just a stone's throw away. If the camp managers at Peterson Bridge continue to be as amiable as they have been in the past, you can always ask if they can drive you down to the tent sites in the camp golf cart.

A short drive to the south on M-37/Grandview Highway is the **Pine River Paddlesports Center** (9590 S. Grandview Highway; 231-862-3471, thepineriver.com). In addition to outfitting families and groups for trips on the Pine River, the center maintains a private campground.

Created with tent-camping families in mind, the campground has established a few rules to ensure guests have a positive experience—in particular, no pets, no fireworks, no loud music, and no foul language. While Peterson Bridge is generally a quiet place to camp, one bad apple can spoil the lot. It's unlikely that you'll have loud, obnoxious neighbors, but if you do, moving to the private campground might save you the disappointment of heading home early.

Peterson Bridge South National Forest Campground

GETTING THERE

From US 131 just south of Cadillac, take Exit 176 for M-115/M-55 West. In 3 miles, bear left (west) at the fork onto M-55. Continue west on M-55 for 18 miles to the four-way stop, and turn left (south) onto M-37; Peterson Bridge is 1.5 miles from the intersection. The campground entrance is on the left (east) side of the road, just south of the bridge.

GPS COORDINATES: N44° 12.117' W85° 48.098'

22

⛺ Silver Creek
State Forest Campground

Beauty ★★★★ Privacy ★★★★ Spaciousness ★★★★★ Quiet ★★★★ Security ★★★★★ Cleanliness ★★★★★

For hiking and paddling, this campground at the confluence of the Pine River and Silver Creek is just the thing.

The Pine River runs through four counties—Osceola, Lake, Wexford, and Manistee. From Edgett's Bridge (about 6.5 miles east-northeast of Luther) to the Low Bridge takeout, the river offers 60 miles of canoeing and fishing. A combination of fast water and easy accessibility make the Pine very popular—so popular, in fact, that before the U.S. Forest Service restricted the number of boats on the water, summer could see 2,000 canoes making the run every week. Visit the Pine River and you'll understand the fuss. You'll also appreciate not seeing so many canoes on the water these days.

A couple of campgrounds get you close to the river. Peterson Bridge South Campground (see previous profile), maintained by the U.S. Forest Service, is one; right off M-37, it has flush toilets and drinking water. Farther upstream, the Michigan Department of Natural Resources operates Lincoln Bridge State Forest Campground. Even farther upstream, where Silver Creek empties into the Pine, is the incomparable Silver Creek State Forest Campground.

The campground offers a mix of sites. On the main loop, there are 19 sites perfect for tents and small trailers. The lots are well manicured, and benches overlook the picturesque

The Pine River comprises 60 miles of paddling and fishing waters spanning four counties.

KEY INFORMATION

CONTACT: Michigan DNR–Baldwin Field Office, 231-745-9465, tinyurl.com /silvercreekcampground

OPEN: Year-round, maintained May–October

SITES: 26

EACH SITE HAS: Picnic table, fire pit

ASSIGNMENT: First come, first served; no reservations

REGISTRATION: Self-register at campground

AMENITIES: Hand-pumped water and vault toilets

PARKING: At sites (or parking area for walk-in sites)

NIGHTLY FEE: $15

ELEVATION: 950'

RESTRICTIONS

PETS: On leash only

FIRES: Fire pits only

ALCOHOL: No stated restrictions; check ahead to confirm

VEHICLES: Michigan Recreation Passport required (see page 8); 2 vehicles/site

OTHER: 6 people/site; 14-day stay limit

Pine River as it flows by. The best of the lot, however, are the seven walk-in sites located on a long, narrow bend in the river. These are spacious and offer plenty of solitude, close enough to the water for you to be lulled to sleep by the sound.

An interesting adventure around the Pine River can be had by hiking or biking the 4-mile Silver Creek Pathway. The pathway passes right through the campground, entering near site 10 and leaving by way of a scenic bridge over the Pine River. It continues up one side of the river and back down the other. The loop is kept separate from the area's off-road-vehicle trails, though you might hear the whine of motors echo through the woods from time to time.

A chief reason to camp at the Silver Creek campground is the Pine River. A significant tributary of the Manistee, the Pine has a solid reputation in the state among paddlers and anglers. Paddlers come for the 7% river grade, which makes this the fastest-flowing water (on average) in the Lower Peninsula. Fast runs and tight turns and some Class I and II rapids thrill beginning paddlers, giving them stories to tell later on of that time they faced down real danger and lived to paddle another day. And depending on how green you are when it comes to paddling, the river can be a challenge and shouldn't be taken lightly. But experienced whitewater canoeists and kayakers will find the ride to be more of an obstacle course than a roller coaster. Scattered boulders and seasonal tree falls add to the negotiations.

Designated a National Wild and Scenic River, the Pine takes you deep into the national forest. Surrounded by cedars, mixed hardwoods, and pines, you can easily lose yourself in the experience—that is, when you're not watching the river for the next banked turn. While the entire 20-plus-mile run from Silver Creek would leave paddlers on the water for a good part of the day (likely more than 8 hours), you're never more than about 4 or 5 miles from the next access point, road, or bridge.

The Pine is also an official Blue Ribbon Trout Stream. This honor is bestowed on rivers for their quality of water, their accessibility, and the ability of fishery to support itself through natural reproduction. The Pine has some of the coldest water among Lower Peninsula rivers. Trout love it, and fly rods and fishing line should be included among the obstacles paddlers have to deal with.

From approximately Memorial Day weekend to Labor Day weekend, the U.S. Forest Service requires a watercraft permit for boats on the Pine River Corridor. The corridor begins at Elm Flats and ends at the Low Bridge Landing, just before the river enters Tippy Pond. You don't need a permit at nearby Lincoln Bridge State Forest Campground, but you do need one at all access points downstream, which are within the protected stretch of river. The permits are free, though there's a $2 reservation fee, and I wouldn't count on getting a permit without a reservation. They can be reserved by calling, visiting, or sending a letter to the Baldwin/White Cloud Ranger Station (231-745-4631) or the Cadillac/Manistee Ranger Station (231-723-2211).

Silver Creek State Forest Campground

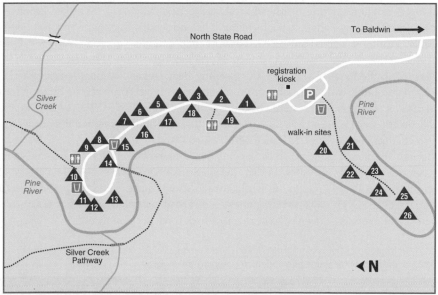

GETTING THERE

From US 10 in Baldwin, take M-37 North for 11 miles to Hermit Road (aka Old M-63), and turn right (east). In 8 miles, turn left (north) onto North State Road. In 4 miles, just shy of East 9 Mile Road, look for the campground on the left (west) side of the road. The signs are pretty clear, but if you come to Lincoln Bridge State Forest Campground, you've gone a mile too far.

GPS COORDINATES: N44° 06.878' W85° 41.005'

23

⚠ Sleeping Bear Dunes National Lakeshore: D. H. DAY CAMPGROUND

Beauty ★★★★★ Privacy ★★★★ Spaciousness ★★★★★ Quiet ★★★★ Security ★★★★ Cleanliness ★★★★★

Campers and day-users come to this sheltered beach for the great views of Sleeping Bear Dunes to the west and Pyramid Point to the east, bookending Lake Michigan and the Manitou Islands.

At the base of the Leelanau Peninsula, you'll find one of the state's most dramatic features, Sleeping Bear Dunes, rising nearly 460 feet above Lake Michigan. North of Empire, the South Dune Highway winds through rolling hills and woods thick with maples, beeches, basswoods, and pines. Small inland lakes dot the map, and it is a great drive in the fall when colors are at their peak.

Nestled in the heart of this area, the Sleeping Bear Dunes National Lakeshore's D. H. Day Campground is easily accessible from the short road that connects the thriving tourist town of Glen Arbor and the restored historical village of Glen Haven. The state government established the campground as a state park in 1920. Day not only donated the property, but he also chaired Michigan's State Park Commission.

Because the campground is part of Sleeping Bear Dunes National Lakeshore, the National Park Service maintains the sites. In fact, the NPS maintains two campgrounds here. The larger of the two, Platte River to the south, attracts more campers and has paved roads and modern facilities. D. H. Day's rustic facilities—a dirt road, pit toilets, and hand-pumped well water—are not enough, however, to keep the crowds away in the summer.

Located far from sources of urban light pollution, Sleeping Bear Dunes National Lakeshore offers amazing opportunities for stargazing and photographing the night sky.

Photo: Jeremy M. White/National Park Service (public domain)

KEY INFORMATION

CONTACT: Sleeping Bear Dunes National Lakeshore, 231-334-4634, nps.gov/slbe; reservations: 877-444-6777, recreation .gov/camping/campgrounds/259242

OPEN: April–late November

SITES: 82

EACH SITE HAS: Picnic table and fire pit

ASSIGNMENT: First come, first served or by reservation (required May–mid-October)

REGISTRATION: Online or by phone; pay at campground office or at its automated pay station, which accepts cash and credit cards

AMENITIES: Hand-pumped potable water and pit toilets

PARKING: At sites

NIGHTLY FEE: $20, plus $25 entrance/ parking pass (good for 7 days)

ELEVATION: 596'

RESTRICTIONS

PETS: On leash only

FIRES: Fire pits only

ALCOHOL: No stated restrictions; check ahead to confirm

VEHICLES: 2/site

OTHER: 6 people/site; quiet hours 10 p.m.– 6 a.m.; camping on tent pads only

---

The campground lies along the shore of Lake Michigan's Sleeping Bear Bay. A path at one end leads to the wide sandy beach. Campers and day users come to this sheltered beach for the great views of Sleeping Bear Dunes to the west and Pyramid Point to the east, book-ending Lake Michigan and the Manitou Islands.

Campers will find relatively level ground at every site. And though the sites aren't as private as some might prefer, they have plenty of room for you to stretch out and enough trees to offer the illusion of seclusion. Generator use is limited to sites 1–31 (for limited hours), so tent campers can enjoy the quiet throughout the remainder of the campground. Group camping is available about a mile away off of M-109 (really a different campground altogether).

Off the main loop, and slightly elevated, sites 57–61 sit a short walk from the water and far from the flow of traffic. Day visitors and campers with an extra vehicle park in a designated overflow parking area next to site 57, but it still seems nicely set apart.

A combination of sand and prevailing westerly winds formed the dunes a couple thousand years ago. The tallest dunes here sit atop limestone plateaus (geologists call this type of dune a perched dune). Like many natural wonders, the forces that created Sleeping Bear cannot be tamed. The dunes here continue to migrate, and significant changes happen over decades and centuries, not millennia and eons.

The federal government established the Sleeping Bear Dunes National Lakeshore, a 72,000-acre national park stretching along 35 miles of Lake Michigan, in 1970. The park incorporates two campgrounds on the mainland and three truly rustic sites on South Manitou Island (highlighted in the next profile). Backcountry campers can pitch a tent throughout the park and on North Manitou Island, with a permit.

A trip to Sleeping Bear Dunes begins at the Philip A. Hart Visitor Center in Empire, at the intersection of M-22 and M-72; here you can learn about the park's numerous hiking trails, the Dune Climb, and the Pierce Stocking Scenic Drive. Built by lumberman Pierce Stocking before the park was even a park, this 7.5-mile loop has numerous overlooks, with views inland toward the picturesque D. H. Day farm and Glen Lake, as well as a short hike to stand 450 breathtaking feet over Lake Michigan.

Tourists climb up and down a popular dune overlook.   *Photo: Benjamin Simeneta/Shutterstock*

At the visitor center, you can purchase the vehicle permit necessary for touring the park (and camping), and the staff can give you directions to the D. H. Day Campground, the northern counterpart to the larger, more modern Platte River Campground.

David Henry Day, the park's namesake, was a relative latecomer to the Sleeping Bear region of Michigan. When he arrived in 1878, the towns of Glen Haven and Glen Arbor were already here. The lumber industry brought cordwood, which steamships used to power their engines, making Glen Haven one of the busiest stops on the Great Lakes.

Day arrived as the supply of lumber was in decline. With astute foresight, he developed other businesses, buying up portions of Glen Haven in the process. He ran the general store and built the cannery nearby that has served as a fruit-processing plant, a warehouse, and now a boat museum. He also bought up vast acreage, much of which he later donated to the state.

In the summer, especially for weekend stays, campers line up in the morning for one of the first-come, first-served sites. Partly because of this, I enjoy visiting after Labor Day. If you enjoy fall camping, the park can seem nearly abandoned this time of year, and it makes a great base camp for exploring fall colors here and farther north into the Leelanau Peninsula.

Several excellent trails can be found at Sleeping Bear; many climb the dunes that offer spectacular views. One of the most popular, the Dunes Trail, begins just up the road at the Dune Climb and continues about 1.5 miles out to a view of Lake Michigan.

Sleeping Bear Dunes National Lakeshore: D. H. Day Campground

GETTING THERE

From US 131 North in Fife Lake Township, turn left onto M-113, following it north and west for 16.5 miles; then turn right (north) onto M-37, and drive 8.1 miles. In Chums Corner, keep straight and continue 7 miles north on US 31, which dead-ends at Grandview Parkway in Traverse City. Turn left onto Grandview Parkway and, in 0.6 mile, turn left (west) onto M-72. In 13 miles, bear right to continue north on M-72; drive 1.1 miles, and turn left to continue west on M-72. In 8.4 miles, M-72 dead ends at the intersection with M-22 in Empire (you'll pass the Philip A. Hart Visitor Center on your right just before the road ends). Turn right (north) onto M-22, and follow it 7.8 miles to Glen Arbor; then turn left (west) onto M-109. The campground entrance is about 1.5 miles ahead, on the right (north) side of the road.

GPS COORDINATES: N44° 53.766' W86° 01.206'

24

⛺ Sleeping Bear Dunes National Lakeshore: SOUTH MANITOU ISLAND, WEATHER STATION CAMPGROUND

Beauty ★★★★★ Privacy ★★★★ Spaciousness ★★★★★ Quiet ★★★★★ Security ★★★★★
Cleanliness ★★★★★

The campground faces south with a fantastic view of the Sleeping Bear Dunes across the water.

If you visit the historical town of Glen Haven, just west of D. H. Day Campground in Sleeping Bear Dunes National Lakeshore (see previous profile), you can tour the old Life Saving Service Station, which is now the Coast Guard Station Maritime Museum. The demonstrations here are pretty interesting. They put on a reenactment of the breeches buoy rescue, complete with the firing of the Lyle gun; this complex drill creates a zip line of sorts between a ship that has run aground and the shore, allowing sailors a way to land without jumping into stormy seas. From Glen Haven, the Manitou Islands are clear on the horizon, and the museum does a great job of highlighting the dangers of the Manitou Passage and the lives of the men who tried to make it a bit safer.

People camp on both North and South Manitou Islands. North Manitou is all wilderness, a backpacker's heaven. With the exception of the ranger station, which offers potable water, you're on your own out here. South Manitou, on the other hand, is slightly more developed. Day visitors stay for a few hours and hike a little or take a motorized tour of the island. For overnight guests, the park maintains three rustic campgrounds. Bay Campground is the closest to the ferry dock and ranger station, which are a mile south. Facing

From the national lakeshore, South Manitou Island is on the horizon to the right.

Photo: Michael J. White © 2019

KEY INFORMATION

CONTACT: Sleeping Bear Dunes National Lakeshore, 231-326-5134, nps.gov/slbe

OPEN: Ferry runs early May–mid-October; rates and reservations: 231-256-9061, manitoutransit.com

SITES: 20

EACH SITE HAS: Fire pits shared by groups of sites

ASSIGNMENT: First come, first served; no reservations

REGISTRATION: Pay for camping and park permit at ferry office

AMENITIES: Water and pit toilets

PARKING: At the dock in Leland

NIGHTLY FEE: $10 for camping; $15/person walk-in fee (in lieu of $25 vehicle permit required elsewhere in the park)

ELEVATION: 599'

RESTRICTIONS

PETS: Prohibited

FIRES: Fire pits only

VEHICLES: NA

ALCOHOL: No stated restrictions; check ahead to confirm

OTHER: 4 people/site

---

east, campers get a view of the Leelanau Peninsula. At the north end of the island, campers walk 3.5 miles from the ranger station to Popple Campground. The site is bare-bones: just seven sites, no potable water, a vault toilet, and (from what I hear) plenty of poison ivy.

The Weather Station Campground lies along the south shore of the island and represents a balance between the other two campgrounds. Farther from the dock but not so rustic as to be uncomfortable, the campground faces south with a fantastic view of the Sleeping Bear Dunes across the water. Prevailing winds here blow from the south, which helps a little during fly season. The sites are tucked in the woods, back from the path. Those along the lake side of the trail have easy access to several paths leading down to the beach. Random groupings of sites share community fire pits.

The island itself has a lot to explore. People have lived on the island for eons. Paleo-Indians hunted here well over 12,000 years ago. More-recent peoples, such as the Ojibwa, camped here as part of their seasonal migrations. The wide, crescent-shaped bay on the island's east edge made the perfect harbor for ships. And loggers, who were looking for wood to sell to fire steamship engines, found a plentiful supply close to one of the busiest shipping lanes on the Great Lakes. A lighthouse was built to warn ships off the island's shallow point. And soon homesteaders came and tried to make a go of farming.

The ruins of old homesteads, the Island Schoolhouse, several cemeteries, and the lighthouse complex could keep you occupied for a day. A rare stand of white cedars grows in the Valley of the Giants in the island's southwest corner. Some of these trees are more than 500 years old. Why they were spared the lumbermen's saw is a mystery, though some suggest that centuries of sand are embedded in the layers of bark, which would quickly dull any blade and make the task of cutting them down not worth the effort.

Along the west shore of the island lies a long perched dune: the Bluffs. From atop this sandy mountain, hikers can see the entirety of the island and Lake Michigan all around. It is even said that on the clearest of days, you can see Wisconsin 40 miles to the west. A trail traverses 3 miles of this rise and is well worth the effort. In terms of hiking, many people will hike the beach around the entire island. The trek is all of 14 miles, but it's easy walking. If the water is at a level that allows you to walk on slightly firmer sand, a motivated and energetic hiker can complete the circumference in a day.

Just off the southern shore of the island, not far from the Weather Station Campground, the dangers of the Manitou Passage are clearly illustrated. Visible from the beach, above the water, is the ruined freighter *Francisco Morazan,* just one of 16 shipwrecks found in the Manitou Passage Underwater Preserve. Kayakers often paddle out to the rusting hulk for a closer view. And this isn't the only shipwreck you can see from a kayak. *The Three Brothers* off Sandy Point is a 160-foot steamer that sank in 1911. It lies in water 5–45 feet deep.

The Manitou Island Transport ferry out of Leland will take you to and from North and South Manitou Islands. You can take your own vessel, and some have even paddled, but this isn't a trip for the novice. Sudden storms in the passage are legendary—one 19th-century explorer recorded the loss of 50 canoes paddled by American Indians making the crossing from Sleeping Bear to the islands.

Sleeping Bear Dunes National Lakeshore: South Manitou Island, Weather Station Campground

GETTING THERE

From US 31 in Traverse City, take M-22 North for 16 miles to Suttons Bay; then turn left (west) onto Race Street/East Duck Lake Road (M-204), and follow it 7.2 miles until it dead-ends at M-22. Turn right (north) onto M-22 and, in 2.2 miles, turn left on River Street in Leland. The Manitou Island Transit office is on the dock at the end of Fishtown.

GPS COORDINATES: N45° 00.072' W86° 06.864'

25

Wilderness State Park:
LAKESHORE CAMPGROUND

Beauty ★★★★★ Privacy ★★★ Spaciousness ★★★★ Quiet ★★★★ Security ★★★★★ Cleanliness ★★★★★

The cedar trees here are thick, and several tents can sit toward the back of these sites and enjoy privacy lacking elsewhere in the campground.

Just west of the Straits of Mackinac, Waugoshance Point juts out into Lake Michigan. The name *Waugoshance* likely comes from the Potawatomi-Ottawa word for "fox," perhaps suffixed with the French word *anse*, or "bay." Interestingly, sailors on the Great Lakes referred to the point as Wobble Shanks. This thin arm of land wraps Sturgeon Bay to the south, and from off the tip of the point, several small, uninhabited islands extend into the passage between the mainland and the Beaver Island Archipelago. This can be a treacherous stretch of water for ships, and those that avoid it tend to follow a path along the northern and western shores of Lake Michigan.

Wilderness State Park includes the entire point. All told, the park has 10,512 acres of woods and 26 miles of coastline along Lake Michigan. There are miles of trails for hiking and biking, islands to explore for sea kayakers, excellent beaches for swimming, good fishing for smallmouth bass off Waugoshance Point, and secluded wilderness cabins on the water for a more sheltered visit.

They don't call it Lakeshore Campground for nothing: the Lake Michigan shoreline here is gorgeous.

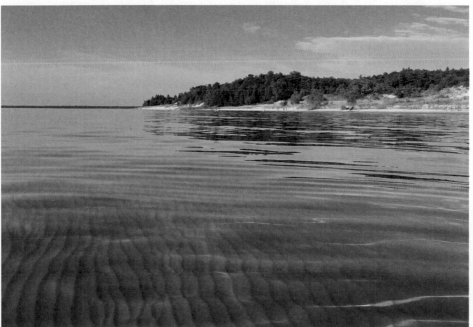

Photo: Frank Wulfers

KEY INFORMATION

CONTACT: Michigan DNR–Wilderness State Park, 231-436-5381, michigan.gov/wilderness; reservations: 800-447-2757, midnrreservations.com

OPEN: Early April–November

SITES: 150

EACH SITE HAS: Picnic table and fire pit

ASSIGNMENT: Online or by phone

REGISTRATION: At park office

AMENITIES: Electricity, water, and flush toilets

PARKING: At sites

NIGHTLY FEE: $33 ($25 off-season)

ELEVATION: 597'

RESTRICTIONS

PETS: On leash only

FIRES: Fire pits only

ALCOHOL: Permitted

VEHICLES: Michigan Recreation Passport required (see page 8); 2 vehicles/site

OTHER: 6 people/site; 15-day stay limit

The park maintains two facilities for camping (well, really one big, divided facility): the Pines Campground and the Lakeshore Campground. Both are in the vicinity of Big Stone Bay, but the former sits back in pine woods, away from the shore. When recommending a state park to tent campers, there's always some risk. The campgrounds at Wilderness are modern—which translates to flush toilets, water, and electricity. Paved roads run through both camps, and the Pines features paved spurs, a playground, a dining hall, and bunkhouses. The risk is that these places are perfect for RVs, motor homes, fifth-wheel trailers, and the like. A state park official told me that the farther north you go in the state, the fewer of these mobile abodes you typically find in camp. Anecdotally, this appears to be true, but if only one RV pulls into camp with a loud generator and air-conditioning unit and parks next to your tent, it is too many. That said, and with all the risks known, I would recommend pitching your tent at the park's Lakeshore Campground.

Lakeshore sits on Big Stone Bay, overlooking Lake Michigan. The campground has 150 sites, and the beach out front attracts campers from the Pines Campground's other 100 sites. This is the kind of place where families come for a week. Their children befriend each other on the beach or hang around the vending machine and spend their days walking around in chummy clumps.

The road through camp is essentially one big, flat loop intersected by the road from the camp entrance (essentially making a long crazy-eight). Each half of the campground has modern restrooms (no showers) and drinking water. The individual sites are less uniform here than at the Pines, and campers park their vehicles on gravel-and-packed-dirt spurs. All in all, this lends the campground a more rustic feel than its well-groomed neighbor.

Sites on the inside of the loops back up to each other, and common sense will tell you that the best spots are either those facing the lake or those toward the back of camp against the woods. Of the wooded sites, I think those along the west corner—sites 116, 117, and 120—are the best. The cedar trees here are thick, and several tents can sit toward the back of these sites and enjoy privacy lacking elsewhere in the campground. Those on the water offer the best views, but they come with a price: little cover from the surrounding trees (that is, little privacy), and the beach is the most popular spot in the park, so these sites see more traffic than most. If you come with properly pitched expectations, tent camping at Wilderness can be quite pleasant.

The park itself offers a world of outdoor recreation. With nearly 23 miles of trails to choose from, including a portion of the North Country Trail, hikers can spend days here far from the developed parts of the park. For water sports, sea kayakers will often put in at the end of Park Drive. From here, it's a 3.5-mile round-trip to the tip of the point. West of the point, you will find Temperance Island and Waugoshance Island. Consult a good paddling guide before making this trip. This close to the Straits of Mackinac, you will often see warnings similar to that posted near the campground beach: Paddlers: Beyond the Protection of Big Stone Bay, Currents Dangerous. It is here that Lake Michigan narrows dramatically and flows into Lake Huron.

Historically, the Straits of Mackinac were some of the first places settled by Europeans. Settlements and forts set up at the tip of the mitt and on Mackinac Island and St. Ignace served fur traders and trappers mining the region's abundant wildlife. A cluster of historical state parks in the area helps visitors really experience this aspect of the straits. The closest would be the Colonial Michilimackinac State Historic Park and Old Mackinac Point Lighthouse. Farther afield, you have Mill Creek State Historic Park and Mackinac Island State Park. All of these could take the better part of the day, and they're great fun with kids.

Wilderness State Park: Lakeshore Campground

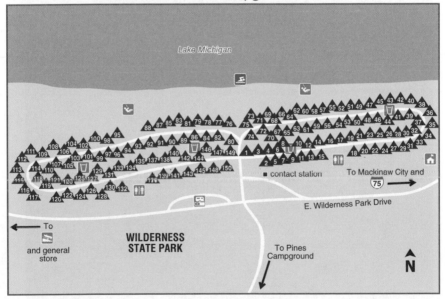

GETTING THERE

In Mackinaw City, take Exit 337 (Nicolet Street) off I-75 North, and turn left at the end of the ramp. In 0.3 mile, turn right (north) on Trails End Road. In 2.3 miles, the road makes a sharp left and becomes East Wilderness Park Drive. Continue south and then west on this road for 7.6 miles into the park; Lakeshore Campground will be on the right (north) side of the road.

GPS COORDINATES: N45° 44.742' W84° 53.994'

NORTHEAST MICHIGAN

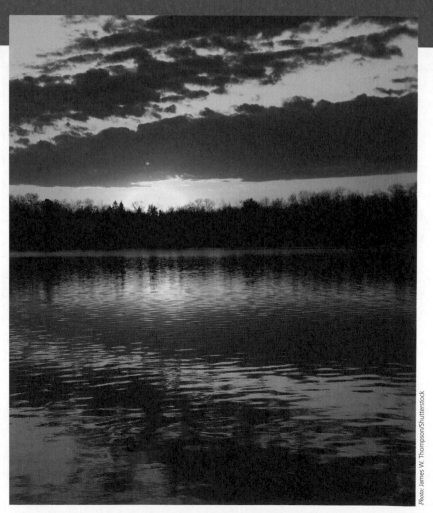

A beautiful sunset at Rifle River Recreation Area (see Campground 31, page 108)

Canoe Harbor
State Forest Campground

Beauty ★★★★ Privacy ★★★ Spaciousness ★★★★ Quiet ★★★★ Security ★★★★★ Cleanliness ★★★★★

Access to the South Branch of the Au Sable River makes this campground attractive to paddlers and anglers alike.

Every year during the last full weekend in July, close to 100 canoes take to the Au Sable River in Grayling. Paddlers carry their boats down to the water just before 9 p.m. By the following morning, 14–19 hours later, they cross a finish line in Oscoda, 130 miles downstream. This is the legendary AuSable River Canoe Marathon; since its inception in 1947, it has become one of the country's premier canoe-racing events. As the paddlers prepare for the race, the city of Grayling celebrates with the AuSable River Festival, featuring arts and crafts, pancake breakfasts, and fun runs. And the morning after the paddlers hit the water, a mass of cyclists takes off from town, trying to beat the paddlers to the finish.

All of this takes place during one week in July. The rest of the year, Grayling and the Au Sable River still draw paddlers and tubers (and anglers) from all over. Most of these visitors take a more leisurely approach to enjoying the water. Whether it involves spending the day lying back on an inner tube, going with the flow, or waking before sunrise to claim a choice stretch of water for laying out a hand-tied fly, camping on the river offers a more intimate experience of the Au Sable.

This grand event is missed by the campers at the Canoe Harbor State Forest Campground, located a half-dozen miles south of the Au Sable on the river's South Branch. The main branch

A native of the forests around Grayling, Kirtland's warbler has rebounded from near-extinction.

Photo: Caleb Putram (public domain)

KEY INFORMATION

CONTACT: North Higgins Lake State Park, 989-821-6125, tinyurl.com/canoeharbor

OPEN: Year-round though not plowed in winter

SITES: 41 (plus 4 canoe group sites)

EACH SITE HAS: Picnic table and fire pit

ASSIGNMENT: First come, first served; no reservations

REGISTRATION: Self-register at campground

AMENITIES: Hand-pumped water and vault toilets

PARKING: At sites

NIGHTLY FEE: $15

ELEVATION: 1,128'

RESTRICTIONS

PETS: On leash only

FIRES: Fire pits only

ALCOHOL: Permitted

VEHICLES: Michigan Recreation Passport required (see page 8); 2 vehicles/site

OTHER: 6 people/site; 15-day stay limit

has its share of campgrounds, many popular with canoe liveries as places to drop off or pick up clients. The boat launches on the Au Sable see a lot of traffic on summer weekends.

Canoe Harbor has its share of traffic but is nonetheless a quieter alternative. There are group sites for campers who arrive by canoe, but drive-in visitors have their pick of 41 spacious sites. Each has a fire pit and picnic table. Tall pines and mixed hardwoods provide shade for most of the sites.

Folks without a boat or rod might be interested to note that the Mason Tract Pathway passes through the campground. From the trailhead near M-72, the trail meanders 9.6 miles to Chase Bridge Road. It more or less charts a parallel path to the river. The trail makes a short loop around the campground, if you're just looking for an easy way to get down to the water.

On the off chance that the campground is full, you can always check the campgrounds on the Au Sable proper. Burton's Field and Keystone Landing State Forest Campgrounds are a short drive (or paddle) away, on the south side of the river. If these are full, which seems unlikely unless you've come up during the canoe marathon, drive a ways west of Grayling on M-72. The state forest maintains a number of nice campgrounds on the Manistee River. Or you could always follow the Au Sable east. From Grayling to Lake Erie, the river hosts quite a few campgrounds operated by the Au Sable State Forest and the Huron National Forest.

The Au Sable is an iconic Michigan river, excellent for paddling and fishing. Upstream from Grayling (a town named for a type of salmon that used to thrive, but is no longer found, in the Au Sable), the river sees fewer canoes. Paddling is more of a wrestling match in this narrower, shallower, and overgrown portion of the river, though some will rise to the challenge. From Grayling and on downstream, the river swarms with paddlers, tubers, and anglers (especially during summer weekends). Fly-fishermen in particular hold the stretch of water from Burton's Landing to the Wakely Bridge in high regard. Nearly 9 miles of the river, known simply as the Holy Waters, are set aside for fly-fishing, with a strict catch-and-release policy. The river here is wide and wadable. It hasn't needed to be stocked in years and naturally supports a strong fishery of trout—mostly brown and brook trout, with a decent population of rainbow.

Downstream, the 23 miles from Mio to the Alcona Dam Pond are designated as the Au Sable National Wild and Scenic River. Established as such in 1984, this section of river has some of the best brown-trout fishing in the Midwest, and paddlers count it among the country's best canoeing.

The closest town, of course, is Grayling. Just north of where US 127 merges with I-75, tourists from the central and eastern parts of the state pass through Grayling and support a strip of fast-food joints and some decent mom-and-pop restaurants downtown. The local economy depends in large part on these travelers, but the military also contributes considerably. Camp Grayling, the largest National Guard training center in the country, takes up huge tracts of land southwest and northeast of town. More than 20,000 people come here for training each year. The rules for exploring land on the Camp Grayling Military Reservation are different from those for the state forest, so if you find yourself roaming off the beaten path, keep an eye out for signs.

Canoe Harbor Forest Campground

GETTING THERE

Take Exit 254 off I-75 North in Grayling, and continue north 0.6 mile; then turn right (east) onto M-72. Continue 12.5 miles, and turn right (south) onto Canoe Harbor Road; the campground is less than a mile ahead, on your left.

GPS COORDINATES: N44° 36.401' W84° 28.173'

27

⚘ Jones Lake State Forest Campground

Beauty ★★★★ Privacy ★★★ Spaciousness ★★★★ Quiet ★★★ Security ★★★★ Cleanliness ★★★★★

About 14 miles northeast of Grayling, Jones Lake offers excellent camping close to the Au Sable River.

At the end of the day, a successful camping trip is one where everyone can find something to keep themselves occupied. Maybe the camp stove ran out of fuel, the ice in the cooler melted, and you had to eat dry cereal all week. Maybe the dog got skunked. Maybe it rained and the tent leaked. All of these make for great stories to tell over future campfires. On the other hand, if campers in your party spend the week whining about being bored, you'll come home only with a lesson learned—even if what you learned is who not to take camping next time.

With this in mind, Jones Lake State Forest Campground presents a bit of a challenge. The campground sits on the southeastern shore of Jones Lake, a fine body of water. A total of 42.5 acres of natural lake empties directly into the East Branch of the Au Sable River. At its deepest, the lake only goes 37 feet, but having been stocked since the middle of the last century, Jones Lake is a good fishing destination. Anglers regularly land largemouth bass,

If you love to fish as well as camp, Jones Lake is the place for you.   *Photo:* Ari A./thedyrt.com

KEY INFORMATION

CONTACT: Michigan DNR–Hartwick Pines State Park, 989-348-7068, tinyurl.com/joneslakecampground

OPEN: Year-round, maintained May–October

SITES: 42

EACH SITE HAS: Picnic table, fire pit

ASSIGNMENT: First come, first served; no reservations

REGISTRATION: Self-register at campground

AMENITIES: Hand-pumped water and vault toilets

PARKING: At sites

NIGHTLY FEE: $15

ELEVATION: 1,216'

RESTRICTIONS

PETS: On leash only

FIRES: Fire pits only

ALCOHOL: No stated restrictions; check ahead to confirm

VEHICLES: Michigan Recreation Passport required (see page 8); 2 vehicles/site

OTHER: 6 people/site; 14-day stay limit

northern pike, and walleye in addition to the usual bluegill and sunfish. Gas motors are not permitted on the lake, but electric trolling motors are allowed. Many folks simply cast a line from shore or wade near the perimeter.

The campground's 42 sites are organized into six loops. Loops 5 and 6 back up onto County Road 612. It's not a busy highway, but there is more traffic noise in this part of the camp than any other. The remaining loops front the lake. I think Loop 3 is the best of the lot, particularly if you can land a site on the water side of the circle. Of course, drinking water and toilets are less convenient to these sites, but they're worth the sacrifice.

The campground doesn't offer much in the way of recreation if fishing isn't your thing (no hiking trails pass through, for example). But there is an impressive state park just a few miles away. The largest state park in the Lower Peninsula, Hartwick Pines offers a full complement of outdoor activities, including hiking, biking, geocaching, and interpretive programs. The visitor center teaches guests about the state's lumber industry, and a logging museum commemorates that industry's history. The centerpiece of the park, however, is the Old Growth Forest Trail. It's one of the park's shortest trails—only 1.25 miles—but it takes you through 85 acres of old-growth forest. That's 85 acres of virgin white pine, the largest such stand of trees in the Lower Peninsula.

The trail is paved and accessible to wheelchairs and strollers. Beneath the towering canopy of trees, the woods are shady and generally cool. In the middle of the forest is the Chapel in the Pines. Erected in 1952, the hand-built chapel is a popular place for small weddings, though it primarily serves as a spot for visitors to rest and contemplate the trees.

Those interested in a longer walk should check out the Weary Legs Trail. Hikers have opportunities along the way to make a shorter loop, but those who go all the way will walk 7.5 miles through woods and a large swath of stump fields.

The state park is responsible for maintaining the campground at Jones Lake—a welcome change from the days when the forest campground was under the management of the local field office—but Hartwick Pines also has a modern campground of its own with 100 sites. The road through the campground is paved, as are the parking areas at each site. If you're OK with campers and RVs, hot showers, and flush toilets, then this just might be the place for you.

Jones Lake State Forest Campground

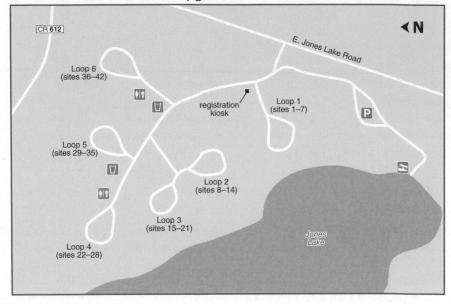

GETTING THERE

From I-75 north of Grayling, take Exit 259 for M-93 East. Continue 6 miles; then turn right (east) onto West County Road 612. After 3 miles, turn right (south) onto East Jones Lake Road. The campground entrance is less than 0.25 mile ahead, on your right.

GPS COORDINATES: N44° 46.957' W84° 35.263'

28

Ocqueoc Falls
State Forest Campground

Beauty ★★★★ Privacy ★★★★ Spaciousness ★★★★★ Quiet ★★★★★ Security ★★★★★ Cleanliness ★★★★

Close your eyes, dangle your feet in the water, and contemplate the quiet current of geological circumstances that created this place.

North of the Mackinac Bridge, Michigan is a land of waterfalls. From Tahquamenon to Bond, the Upper Peninsula is flush with falling waters. South of Big Mac, however, it's slim pickings. Ocqueoc is the only named waterfall in the Lower Peninsula. (There is one unnamed falls. On a small stream that feeds the Manistee River, it's less accessible and not as picturesque.) According to some sources, the name of the river and falls, pronounced "AH-key-ock," meant "crooked river" to the Ojibwa who lived here. Virgil Vogel, the author of *Indian Names in Michigan*, however, says that definition has no basis in the Ojibwa vocabulary. Thus, according to this expert at least, the meaning of the word *Ocqueoc* remains a mystery.

Here, where the often-twisty Ocqueoc River becomes Ocqueoc Falls, the water is edged by a stone bank. Along the rock's weathered top, you can just make out the shapes of fossilized shells . . . or are they some kind of plant? In either case, with little else but kids playing in the falls and some adults wading upstream, it's easy to close your eyes, dangle your feet in the water, and contemplate the quiet current of geological circumstances that created this place.

The Ocqueoc day-use area and campground sit across the road from each other. Arrayed in a single loop, campsites along the campground's west and southwest edges are on the

Ocqueoc Falls lies just north of the campground, across the road.

KEY INFORMATION

CONTACT: Michigan DNR–P. H. Hoeft State Park, 989-734-2543, tinyurl.com /ocqueocfalls

OPEN: Year-round though not plowed in winter

SITES: 15

EACH SITE HAS: Picnic table and fire pit

ASSIGNMENT: First come, first served; no reservations

REGISTRATION: Self-register at campground

AMENITIES: Hand-pumped well water and pit toilets

PARKING: At sites

NIGHTLY FEE: $15

ELEVATION: 706'

RESTRICTIONS

PETS: On leash only

FIRES: Fire pits only

ALCOHOL: No stated restrictions; check ahead to confirm

VEHICLES: Michigan Recreation Passport required (see page 8); 2 vehicles/site

OTHER: 6 people/site; 15-day stay limit

Ocqueoc River. A bluff raises half of the sites slightly above the others. The campground is what you might expect if you're familiar with camping at state forest facilities. There are pit toilets, and you can pump drinkable water from the well.

The sites are mostly grassy, with packed dirt and gravel spurs. Shade comes from a mix of maples, oaks, white pines, and beeches. The first couple of sites on the water, 4 and 5, enjoy the least privacy but have the best views of the river. Sites 7–10 sit on the bluff and, with the exception of site 9, directly overlook the water. If privacy is your thing and being on the water isn't a requirement, sites 12 and 13 were custom-made for you. Found at the far side of the loop, these sites are deep, backing into a wood of tall pines—very spacious and set apart from the rest of the campground.

Waterfalls typically indicate a change in geology that often goes unnoticed on dry land— and a lot is going on geologically in this part of the state. The region's karst topography (also see Tomahawk Creek Flooding, page 114) means that layers of bedrock beneath the surface are slowly eroding. Near Tomahawk and Shoepac Lakes, this has resulted in sinkholes. You can also find sinkholes in Alpena County, and even under the waters of Thunder Bay. Near Ocqueoc, it is said that the Little Ocqueoc River, a tributary of the Ocqueoc, flows underground for a portion of its path, and that at one point one of its branches can be seen flowing out of a hill. The website for the town of Onaway indicates that you can see this for yourself about a mile north of M-68 on Silver Creek Road—this would be just a few miles from the campground, but I've been unable to locate the spot.

But the most fun you can have on the water typically occurs aboveground. Let's begin with the waterfall. The Ocqueoc River drops 5–6 feet at the falls. Certainly no Niagara, the falls are tall enough to be interesting yet short enough that kids can put on some water shoes and wade out into the cascading pools created by the water.

Paddlers camping at the state forest campground find themselves in the middle of the finest water for canoeing and kayaking on the Ocqueoc. The entire length of the river— beginning as far upstream as its source, Lake Emma (17 miles south)—is accessible by boat, especially in the spring, but many folks rent canoes and put in near Millersburg. Between Millersburg and Lake Huron lie 20 miles of river, with plenty of action for intermediate paddlers. Though never producing whitewater, the river does offer some fast technical turns, and at least one section needs to be portaged or waded in low water.

Anglers will find the upper portions of the Ocqueoc are warmer than the sections downstream of the falls. Dams upstream warm the river and support fishery of pike and smallmouth bass. Where cold-water streams feed the river—from the falls to Lake Huron— you will find trout and steelhead.

The campground and day-use area were built in 1976 to commemorate the country's bicentennial. The development included the Bicentennial Pathway, a long loop with two cutbacks, giving you the option of a short, medium, or long hike. The best section for viewing the falls is the shorter of the paths, which comes up just shy of crossing the Little Ocqueoc. Just downstream from the falls, the river drops into a rocky gorge with walls some 20 feet high. This trail takes you by the falls and along this stretch of river. Simply gorgeous.

Open to both hikers and mountain bikers, the longer path takes in the entire 6-mile oblong loop, hemmed in on the west by the river and on the east by Silver Creek Road. With an easy grade, the path is no pushover ride for cyclists—6 miles is 6 miles, after all—but neither will anyone with experience go home with shaky knees and sore thighs.

Ocqueoc Falls State Forest Campground

GETTING THERE

From I-75, take Exit 310 for M-68 East. After about 27 miles (about 8 miles east of Onaway), the road makes a sharp 90-degree turn to the left (north) and then begins to curve right (east) 2.2 miles later—Ocqueoc Falls Highway is just ahead on the left, just as M-68 is coming out of this second turn on its way east. Turn left onto Ocqueoc Falls Highway; the campground and day-use area are less than 0.5 mile away.

GPS COORDINATES: N45° 23.706' W84° 03.378'

29

Ossineke State Forest Campground

Beauty ★★★★★ Privacy ★★★★ Spaciousness ★★★★★ Quiet ★★★★★ Security ★★★★ Cleanliness ★★★★★

If you're looking to leave the world behind, this is your spot.

On a beautiful summer day, as clouds float lazily in front of a bright-blue sky, their shadows dappling the sandy beach at the southern end of Thunder Bay, it's hard to imagine that you're looking out over one of the most dangerous stretches of water in the Great Lakes. Lake Huron is the second largest of these lakes, and sailors making the turn south from the Straits of Mackinac know that it pays to keep a keen eye on the weather.

Ever since René-Robert Cavelier, Sieur de La Salle, began exploring the Great Lakes by sailing ship, wrecking first the *Frontenac* in 1679 and then losing the legendary *Le Griffon* later that year, these freshwater seas have taken thousands of ships, and few spans of water are as treacherous as those off North Point and Thunder Bay Island. To protect the cultural legacy of these wrecks, the area was designated an underwater preserve by the state in 1981. Nineteen years later, an agreement with the National Oceanic and Atmospheric Administration (NOAA) established the Thunder Bay National Marine Sanctuary—jointly managed by the state and NOAA. So far, more than 200 ships have been found within the boundaries of the preserve.

The Ossineke (pronounced "AH-sin-eek") State Forest Campground, a few miles northwest of South Point, overlooks the southern end of Thunder Bay. Neatly tucked between the unincorporated village of Ossineke and the water, the park caps off a section of Lake Huron shoreline that's bordered to the south by Mackinaw State Forest, Negwegon State Park, Au Sable State Forest, and Huron National Forest, all in sprawling succession.

A swale reflects the forest scenery on an overcast day.

Photo: Paul Bruce

KEY INFORMATION

CONTACT: Michigan DNR–P. H. Hoeft State Park, 989-734-2543, tinyurl.com/ossineke

OPEN: Year-round though not plowed in winter

SITES: 42

EACH SITE HAS: Picnic table and fire pit

ASSIGNMENT: First come, first served; no reservations

REGISTRATION: Self-register at campground

AMENITIES: Hand-pumped water and vault toilets

PARKING: At sites

NIGHTLY FEE: $15

ELEVATION: 577'

RESTRICTIONS

PETS: On leash only

FIRES: Fire pits only

ALCOHOL: No stated restrictions; check ahead to confirm

VEHICLES: Michigan Recreation Passport required (see page 8); 2 vehicles/site

OTHER: 6 people/site; 15-day stay limit

From above, the campground looks like an unbalanced mobile. Drive into the park and you come to a T. Turn left to find another T, off of which balances a long road with turn-around loops at each end—here you find sites 1–17 and 18–26. If, on the other hand, you turn right, the main road leads to sites 27–42, with a loop of their own.

Driving in from Ossineke, following the main drive left, you'll first notice a pleasant picnic area with a view of the lake. To the left, sites 1–17 alternate from the water side to the wooded side of the drive. Site 9 is reserved for the campground host. Sites 15 and 17, in particular, enjoy a great view of the bay. Unique to site 15 is the grave marker of one A. J. Michalowsky. In 1865, this 26-year-old man drowned while attempting to sail from Ossineke to Alpena. His body washed up here, and here he was buried—another testament, I suppose, to Shipwreck Alley's dangerous reputation.

To the right of the picnic area, far fewer sites sit on the wooded side of the road—most are on the water. At most sites, stands of pines, cedars, and maples screen the view of the bay, but they also serve to protect campsites from winds off the beach. Here and there, paths cut through to the water.

This is a great campground for swimming—but keep in mind that the Great Lakes are always a bit chilly. The beach is mostly sandy. The water here is shallow, and if you wear lake shoes for the rocks, you can walk quite a ways out into the bay.

Two islands—Scarecrow and Bird—wait on the horizon, a few miles offshore to the east. Kayakers find it an enjoyable paddle to follow the shore of South Point from the Black River in Negwegon State Park. From there, they launch a mile into the lake to Bird Island and then leapfrog to Scarecrow Island. Between these two lies the closest shipwreck to the campground. The *William H. Stevens* rests in 10 feet of water. This 117-foot schooner sank with a cargo hold full of wheat in the fall of 1863. There was no recorded loss of life with this sinking, so any phantom sailors you see wandering the beach at night are merely the result of an overactive imagination.

Ossineke State Forest Campground has one hiking trail, the 1-mile Ossineke Pathway, but with so much state and national forestland around, hikers will find trails enough for exploring. Just to the south, in Negwegon State Park, 11.6 miles of path are spread among three separate trails. The terrain here varies, and paths often pass through boggy swamp-land, so getting your feet wet is not unlikely.

Negwegon is an undeveloped park, and just getting there is a bit of a feat. The main road to the park entrance is the aptly named Sand Hill Road, and officials warn that a four-wheel-drive vehicle is often the only way to get through the road's sandy patches. Once you're in, the park offers potable water, an outhouse, and four backcountry campsites. If you're looking to leave the world behind, this is your spot.

If you're looking for some civilization, Alpena is 12 miles north on US 23. There, you can learn more about the Thunder Bay National Marine Sanctuary by visiting the **Great Lakes Maritime Heritage Center** (500 W. Fletcher St.; 989-356-8805, thunderbay.noaa.gov/maritime/glmhc.html). This maritime museum tells the story of the boats that have gone down near Thunder Bay through detailed exhibits, models of various ships, and a life-size deck that gives visitors the feeling of being aboard a ship in a storm on Lake Huron.

Ossineke State Forest Campground

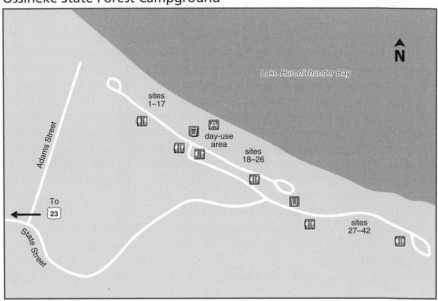

GETTING THERE

From US 23 in Ossineke, 12 miles south of Alpena, head east on Ossineke Road and, after 1 mile, turn right onto State Street. The campground entrance is 0.5 mile ahead at the end of the street.

GPS COORDINATES: N44° 27.342′ W83° 25.139′

30

⛺ Pigeon River State Forest Campground

Beauty ★★★★ Privacy ★★★★★ Spaciousness ★★★★ Quiet ★★★★★ Security ★★★★★ Cleanliness ★★★★★

The state forest—with its hardwoods and pines, grassy clearings and fields, and wetlands— is an ideal environment for Rocky Mountain elk.

Three of Michigan's finest trout waters flow through the Pigeon River Country State Forest: the Sturgeon, Pigeon, and Black Rivers. In the early part of the last century, Ernest Hemingway made his way often to the Black River and spent days casting a line, nights sleeping under the open sky. In his ever-so-concise style, he called this little piece of country "the pine plains east of Vanderbilt."

In 1919 those pine plains were incorporated as a state forest, protecting the last big tract of almost-wild wilderness in the Lower Peninsula. Not quite untouched, Pigeon River Country was logged and left for scrap by lumbermen. Forest fires raged here, the last in 1939. Today, we have 118,000 acres of managed wilderness, complete with a herd of elk comparable to none other this side of the Mississippi.

The state forest has seven rustic campgrounds. Most are on small lakes; one is set aside for equestrian camping. Driving in from Vanderbilt on Sturgeon Valley Road, you pass close by three of them—Pickerel Lake, Pigeon Bridge, and Round Lake. The fourth, however, is the one you want. North on Twin Lakes Road, less than a mile past the Pigeon River Country Field Office, is the Pigeon River State Forest Campground (not to be confused with Pigeon Bridge State Forest Campground).

The campground is on a small bend of the Pigeon River. There are 18 campsites, 15 on a main loop. Sites 1–6 (with the exception of 5) sit right on the water. Sites 7–15 complete the loop. The remaining four sites are a bit removed, east of the main road into the campground.

Section Four Lake is a couple of miles north of the campground in Pigeon River Country State Forest.

Photo: Michael M. Philip

KEY INFORMATION

CONTACT: Michigan DNR–Otsego Lake State Park, 989-732-5485, tinyurl.com /pigeonriver

OPEN: Year-round though not plowed in winter

SITES: 18

EACH SITE HAS: Picnic table and fire pit

ASSIGNMENT: First come, first served; no reservations

REGISTRATION: Self-register at campground

AMENITIES: Artesian well and vault toilets

PARKING: At sites

NIGHTLY FEE: $15

ELEVATION: 887'

RESTRICTIONS

PETS: On leash only (maximum 6')

FIRES: Fire pits only

ALCOHOL: No stated restrictions; check ahead to confirm

VEHICLES: Michigan Recreation Passport required (see page 8); 2 vehicles/site

OTHER: 6 people/site; 15-day stay limit

Site 17 is particularly attractive. The site is right on the water where Ford Lake Road crosses over the Pigeon; there is a notable lack of privacy here, however. There are no trees, it's right on the road, and day visitors "enjoy" an unobstructed view of the parking area.

Sites along the water are more or less grassy. The others are nestled in pine woods, fringed by ash and other hardwoods. These wooded sites are floored with the reddish hue of fallen pine needles.

Water is provided by an ever-flowing artesian well. Two vault toilets are in the middle of the loop; access is easy enough unless you're walking over from sites 17 and 18. It's not terribly far (less than 0.2 mile), just not as convenient.

The 3-mile stretch of the Pigeon River, from Sturgeon Valley Road to the campground, is wide (20–40 feet) and shallow (rarely deeper than 4 feet). This is the first section of the river considered accessible for paddlers—you can paddle a bit upstream, but the river becomes too small and obstructed to enjoy the trip.

Because the water is wide, shallow, and relatively even-bottomed, anglers of all stripes wake early in the morning, don waders, and try their luck catching brown trout and brook trout. Many stay at the campground, though others camp elsewhere and drive in early.

The 80-mile High Country Pathway passes through this campground. Tracing a large loop through portions of Mackinaw and Pigeon River Country State Forests, the trail was designed for hikers looking for a week of backpacking. The pathway connects a number of state forest campgrounds (including Tomahawk Creek Flooding on page 114).

For shorter hikes, the Shingle Mill Pathway offers 6-, 10-, and 11-mile loops. The main trailhead is at Pigeon Bridge, and the trail follows the river for a time. The High Country Pathway connects with a portion of this trail.

In recent years, mountain bikers have secured the right to use the Shingle Mill and High Country Pathways. It took some convincing, but the mountain biking community has developed a reputation for respecting hikers and caring for the trails. In 2006, the International Mountain Biking Association added the High Country Pathway to its list of epics, calling the route a "soul searcher."

A year before the state forest was officially established, seven elk were released into the wild here; because the native elk had become extinct, Rocky Mountain elk were introduced in an attempt to restore a viable herd. The state forest—with its hardwoods and pines, grassy clearings and fields, and wetlands—is an ideal environment for these animals. The elk made themselves at home, and today the herd numbers more than 1,000.

The elk are most active in September, when the bulls are looking to make a name for themselves in the herd—a lot of bugling and playing rough with the brush. Most nature watchers come out on the weekends, so your best bet is to come during the week. Or better yet, come in late April or early May. There are few crowds in the spring, yet the elk are out feasting on fresh vegetation.

The west part of the wilderness is a 6,300-acre no-motor area called Green Timbers. Hiking and cross-country-skiing trails will appeal to some, and hunters make good use of the woods.

In the late 1960s and early 1970s, energy companies began pushing for more access to Pigeon River Country. The presence of oil and gas raised questions about proper land use within a designated wilderness area and led to an extended court battle. In 1979, a Michigan Supreme Court decision led to a compromise allowing for drilling in the southern third of the forest.

Pigeon River State Forest Campground

GETTING THERE

From I-75, take Exit 290 southbound onto Mill Street in Vanderbilt; in 0.5 mile, turn left (east) onto East Main Street/East Sturgeon Valley Road. After 11.5 miles, turn left (north) onto Twin Lakes Road, and drive 1.7 miles to the campground entrance. (About 1.4 miles before Twin Lakes Road, you'll pass Pigeon Bridge State Forest Campground on your left— again, don't get this confused with Pigeon River.) The field office is about 0.5 mile before you reach the campground.

GPS COORDINATES: N45° 10.596' W84° 25.668'

31

⚶ Rifle River State Recreation Area:
SPRUCE CAMPGROUND

Beauty ★★★★★ Privacy ★★★★★ Spaciousness ★★★★★ Quiet ★★★★★ Security ★★★★★
Cleanliness ★★★★★

Here at the end of the road, so to speak, campers get a true sense of the park's wilderness and a great experience of the Rifle River.

In the northern half of the Lower Peninsula, few rivers can live up to the reputation of the Au Sable, celebrated for its beauty as much as its recreational value. This close to the Au Sable, you can see why it's easy to miss another of Michigan's great waterways, the Rifle River. The watershed boundary of these two rivers traces a meandering path through northern Ogemaw County. Once used as a shortcut for running lumber down to mills on Saginaw Bay, the Rifle has become a destination river in its own right.

The river pours out of the lakes and streams of Rifle River State Recreation Area. From there, it flows 47 miles south and east to the bay. Not as grand as its illustrious neighbor, the Rifle offers days of easy paddling and a strong fishery of brown trout and steelhead—perfect for an early morning of fly-fishing or a lazy afternoon float. The nearby campgrounds of the recreation area offer a great base camp for exploring the upper portions of the river or any of the region's other recreational activities—hiking and biking park trails, fishing in nearby lakes and rivers, or relaxing in camp by the water.

White-tailed deer share the recreation area with campers. Other wild residents include rabbits, raccoons, turkeys, grouses, minks, and otters.

Photo: James W. Thompson./Shutterstock

KEY INFORMATION

CONTACT: Michigan DNR–Rifle River State Recreation Area, 989-473-2258, michigan.gov/rifleriver; reservations: 800-447-2757, midnrreservations.com

OPEN: Mid-April–November

SITES: 16

EACH SITE HAS: Picnic table and fire pit

ASSIGNMENT: Online or by phone

REGISTRATION: At park office

AMENITIES: Hand-pumped water and vault toilets

PARKING: At sites

NIGHTLY FEE: $13

ELEVATION: 868'

RESTRICTIONS

PETS: On leash only

FIRES: Fire pits or in waist-high stoves in picnic area only

ALCOHOL: Permitted

VEHICLES: Michigan Recreation Passport required (see page 8); 2 vehicles/site

OTHER: 6 people/site; 15-day stay limit

The recreation area has four campgrounds. As you drive in from the park entrance at its north end, Spruce Campground is the farthest south, nearly 3.5 miles into the park. Nestled in dense woods on the Rifle River, the campground's 16 sites are plotted around a small double loop in sort of a lazy-eight shape. Few sites at Spruce have room enough for a fifth-wheel; in fact, some sites are cozy enough that only the most humble of pop-ups could squeeze in alongside the fire pit. Sites 169 and 172 get you closest to the river, but none are far from the water's edge. Here at the end of the road, so to speak, campers get a true sense of the park's wilderness and a great experience of the Rifle River.

The campground often fills up on the weekends, so plan ahead and make reservations online. If Spruce is full, however, consider one of the park's other campgrounds. Driving into the park, the first you come to is the largest of the pack, Grousehaven. Seventy-five sites, divided into two separate loops, have electric hookups and share modern facilities. Tent campers who appreciate a little luxury should take note of the bathrooms and hot showers at Grousehaven. This is one of the few state parks that keep a modern campground open year-round, and that means heated restrooms in the winter. This is good to know after you've taken an unfortunate dunk in a spring-swollen river or if you simply want to warm up during colder months.

Assuming you haven't come to rent a cabin or camp as a large group, there are just two other campgrounds at Rifle River State Recreation Area, both of them rustic. Devoe Lake Campground has 58 sites on Devoe and Jewett Lakes. Divvied up into seven loops, the campground is rather intimate and doesn't feel as big as it really is.

A half mile farther down the way, 25 sites on the Rifle River make up the Ranch Rustic Campground. The sites here are large enough for fifth-wheel trailers, and a few trees offer shade. That said, bushes and brush between sites act as a screen between neighbors. Nearby, an open field provides plenty of room for throwing a Frisbee or enjoying a sunny picnic, and a footbridge crosses over the Rifle, carrying hikers to the western edge of the park.

Many campers come this way for the fishing. In addition to the Rifle River, which is popular with fly-fishermen and those who like to cast a line off the bridge near the Ranch Campground, the park has a couple of deep lakes, several shallower lakes, and miles of creek to explore. Devoe and Grousehaven Lakes are both more than 50 feet deep. The other ponds and lakes are less than 20 feet. The most popular with boaters, Grousehaven Lake has a decent fishery of perch, rainbow trout, sunfish, and bass.

It's a shame that many visitors to the recreation area will simply stay close to camp or stake out a lake for fishing and not venture much deeper. The park offers a stellar multiuse trail. A particular favorite with hikers and bikers, the Rifle River Trail winds through 14 miles of the park's interior, following the river for a time and tracing the shore of most of the park's lakes. Mountain bikers will find that most of the pedaling is easy, but the north section of the trail offers some technical challenges.

Many paddlers use the recreation area as a base camp for excursions downstream. Closer to the park and the river's headwaters, the water is shallow and the bank can be overgrown, so most folks put in the Rifle River at Sage Lake Road at the south boundary of the park.

Along the way, the water is smooth and slow and poses little challenge to even novice paddlers. Though they can't really be seen (or readily recognized) from the water, two important archaeological sites lie along the banks of the upper Rifle River. On maps, they are labeled "aboriginal earthworks" and can be found just south of Peters and Selkirk Roads.

Rifle River State Recreation Area: Spruce Campground

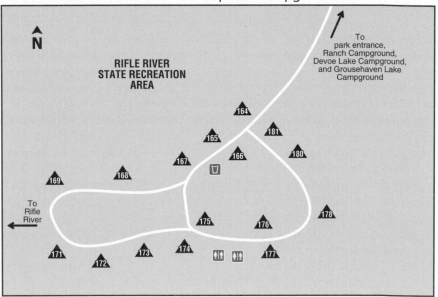

GETTING THERE

In Alger, take I-75 to Exit 202 for M-33. Continue north on M-33 for 20 miles into Rose City, and then turn right onto Main Street, which becomes East Rose City Road. Continue east for 4.7 miles until you see the sign for the park entrance on the right (south) side of the road.

GPS COORDINATES: N44° 23.286' W84° 02.220'

⛺ Sawmill Point Primitive Campsites

Beauty ★★★★★ Privacy ★★★★ Spaciousness ★★★★ Quiet ★★★★★ Security ★★★★ Cleanliness ★★★

Paths from the individual sites lead down to narrow ledges of earth at the water's edge.

The Mio Dam marks a significant change in the Au Sable River. Upstream the watercourse runs unregulated. The Mio Dam, however, widens the river and slows its pace, creating Mio Pond. This dam is the first portage on the Au Sable, and the four dams and four flood ponds that follow create a river that is a far cry from the one paddled by American Indians and early European explorers, or even the loggers who used the river to float their lumber to Lake Huron. Much of this stretch of the Au Sable lies within Huron–Manistee National Forest, and the U.S. Forest Service has made good use of the recreational opportunities these dams create.

The largest of these man-made lakes is Cooke Pond, and high on a bluff overlooking the pond, you'll find the centerpiece of the Huron National Forest: the Lumberman's Monument and Visitor Center. The monument itself is a 14-foot bronze sculpture of three loggers. Erected in 1931, the center was built by the Civilian Conservation Corps, who also planted the large pine trees visitors enjoy today. You may find it ironic that a national forest monument celebrates the industry that harvested most of the state's forests, but logging was a fact of life in northern Michigan, and this visitor center does a great job of telling that story.

Adjacent to the Lumberman's Monument and Visitor Center, people can set up camp at Monument Campground. The sites are rustic, and the campground amenities are limited

The scenic beauty of Cooke Pond as seen from Lumberman's Monument

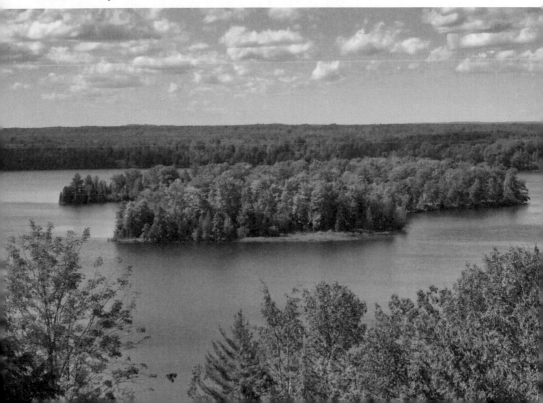

KEY INFORMATION

CONTACT: Huron–Manistee National Forest, Huron Shores Ranger Station; 989-362-8961, tinyurl.com/sawmillpoint; reservations: 877-444-6777, recreation.gov/camping/campgrounds/234130

OPEN: January–November

SITES: 16

EACH SITE HAS: Fire pit

ASSIGNMENT: Reservations required April 15–November 30; first come, first served January 1–April 14

REGISTRATION: Register and pay for camping permit at Lumberman's Monument and Visitor Center

AMENITIES: Hand-pumped water and vault toilets

PARKING: At sites

NIGHTLY FEE: $10 April 15–November 30; free January 1–April 14

ELEVATION: 701'

RESTRICTIONS

PETS: On leash only

FIRES: Fire pits only

ALCOHOL: No stated restrictions; check ahead to confirm

VEHICLES: 2/site

OTHER: 10 people/site; 14-day stay limit

to vault toilets and drinking water. Farther afield, however, a number of primitive sites are available in the form of a dispersed campground. These would be the 42 sites (numbered 32–73) found up and down the length of Cooke Pond. These sites vary in accessibility. On the campground map, sites are coded with a C, D, or W, for canoe, drive-in, or walk-in access, respectively.

For this book, we'll be looking at the 16 drive-in sites that the U.S. Forest Service calls the Sawmill Point Primitive Campsites. But be aware that 26 more sites await campers looking for a little adventure. For example, Horseshoe Island is a popular scenic feature of Cooke Pond, visible from the overlook at the visitor center. Few of the travelers passing through realize, as they take in the sweep of landscape, that they could camp on that idyllic island. Instead, they snap a few photos, round up the kids, and head off for the next stop. The few in the know, however, reserve the campsite ahead of time, make the 1.5-mile paddle out to campsite 41C, and enjoy a unique experience of nature.

Sawmill Point offers a similar experience for campers not able to paddle or hoof it to one of the less accessible sites. The point juts out into Cooke Pond a mile or two downriver from the Lumberman's Monument. The terrain here drops sharply to the pond. You can only imagine how much more impressive these bluffs and valleys must have appeared when the water was at its normal levels. Sites are split between the northeast and southwest sides of the point. Sites 48D–57D edge the northeast side of the point, all from a single road. Sites 42D–47D are on their own loop.

All but two (46D and 47D) of the campground's 16 sites overlook the water. Paths from the individual sites lead down to narrow ledges of earth at the water's edge. It would be hard to lower a canoe to the river from camp, but thankfully the campground has a boat launch. There's an overall shaggy feel to the place, but it's a primitive campground—the vault toilets and hand-pumped water are luxuries—and if you find landscaping important, definitely choose one of the other national forest campgrounds nearby (Monument and Rollways are always good bets). The campground is popular with anglers and others looking for a base close to the water.

This section of the Au Sable River is on the Lumberman's Monument Auto Tour. This scenic 68-mile drive begins at the Tawas Point State Park and makes a crooked loop up to the monument, over to Oscoda, and back to Tawas. Along the way it passes museums, historical markers, and quite a few natural sites. You can pick up a brochure at the state park. One stop on the tour you shouldn't miss is Iargo Springs. Just 3 miles west of the monument on Iargo Road, the springs here were once used by American Indians. During the logging years, lumbermen dammed the springs and diverted the water to their camps. You can follow the water's path toward the river as it flows downhill over a number of man-made dams. It's a 300-step stairway down, so keep in mind that you'll have to walk back up.

While the Au Sable plays a central role in the region's recreational opportunities, there's more here than just paddling. The Highbanks River Trail begins at the main road into Sawmill Point and continues west, following the river. The 6.3-mile route passes the Lumberman's Monument and Canoers Memorial Monument before ending at Iargo Springs. This is a favorite trail with hikers and cross-country skiers.

Sawmill Point Primitive Campsites

GETTING THERE

From US 23 in Oscoda, drive west on West Mill Street, which quickly becomes East River Road and then just River Road; whatever the name, follow the road 14.3 miles. Turn right (north) on Cooke Dam Road; then drive 1.5 miles, and turn left onto Sid Town Road. You're there.

GPS COORDINATES: N44° 27.342' W83° 36.366'

33

Tomahawk Creek Flooding State Forest Campground

Beauty ★★★★ Privacy ★★★ Spaciousness ★★★★ Quiet ★★★★★ Security ★★★★ Cleanliness ★★★★

Few places are as enjoyable for camping as this site, surrounded by thick woods, pleasant water for swimming and fishing, and trails enough for days of hiking.

Southeast of Onaway in Mackinaw State Forest is one of the state's more unique geological features—the Sinkhole Area. The region is dotted with deep wooded sinkholes, small lakes, and a number of nearby rustic state forest campgrounds, including this one on Tomahawk Creek Flooding. Few places are as enjoyable for camping as this site, surrounded by thick woods, pleasant water for swimming and fishing, and trails enough for days of hiking.

That said, the scenery on the drive in from M-33 can be downright discouraging. Tomahawk Lake Highway passes through flat terrain lined with grass and scrubby trees. It might be enough to make you turn around, but fear not: the destination more than makes up for the drive. The campground is south of the "highway" off of Dam Road (1 mile in from M-33). Other campgrounds can be found farther along on Shoepac and Tomahawk Lakes; both are nice spots for camping (though Shoepac seems better suited for fifth-wheel trailers and RVs). On the off-chance that both units at Tomahawk Creek Flooding are full, campers should find a site at one of these excellent alternatives.

Tomahawk Creek Flooding is the largest body of water in this section of the Atlanta State Forest. The campground on the north shore of the man-made lake is actually divided into two sections, the West Unit and the East Unit. Here, we look at the 24 sites that make up the West Unit. On the map, nearly half of these are on the water, but, in reality, some

You may spot small songbirds in the trees and bushes that surround the water.

KEY INFORMATION

CONTACT: Aloha State Park, 231-625-2522, tinyurl.com/tomahawkcreekflooding

OPEN: Year-round though not plowed in winter

SITES: 24 (West Unit)

EACH SITE HAS: Picnic table and fire pit

ASSIGNMENT: First come, first served; no reservations

REGISTRATION: Self-register at campground

AMENITIES: Hand-pumped water and vault toilets

PARKING: At sites

NIGHTLY FEE: $15

ELEVATION: 856'

RESTRICTIONS

PETS: On leash only

FIRES: Fire pits only

ALCOHOL: Permitted

VEHICLES: Michigan Recreation Passport required (see page 8); 2 vehicles/site

OTHER: 6 people/site; 15-day stay limit

---

have better access than others. Site 22, for example, has a particularly nice view of the lake. That said, there's hardly a bad place to pitch a tent here. With spacious, grassy sites and plenty of shade from pines and the usual assortment of hardwoods, the campground sites offer room to spread out and a decent amount of privacy.

(If your campers are more interested in swimming than fishing, however, the campground on Tomahawk Lake might be a better choice. There's a day-use area with a sandy beach, and some of the campsites are close enough to the shore that you could presumably slip straight from the tent into the water.)

The campground has a boat launch, as do Tomahawk Lake, Little Tomahawk Lake, Shoepac Lake, and Francis Lake. There's no end to the fishing holes anglers might find. Fisheries here boast bluegill and largemouth bass. Off-road vehicles are restricted in the campgrounds themselves, but there is an abundance of trails for the off-road enthusiast.

The state forest's most interesting and scenic features are the sinkholes just north of the Tomahawk Lake Highway. Not only does the 2.5-mile loop offer a pleasant nature hike, but it's also a chance to see geological forces in action.

Campers interested in understanding the geology of the Sinkhole Area will first learn a little about karst topography. This is when a layer of bedrock erodes, causing the ground above it to sink. In the case of northern Michigan, the bedrock is limestone and the ground above it is glacial till. (Glacial till is the sediment that the glacier scraped up as it advanced. When it retreated, it left behind piles of this rubble everywhere. The glaciers really defined the landscape here.)

Groundwater seeps down through the till and eats away at the limestone, which dissolves very easily for a rock. When enough limestone is gone, the foundation collapses. Sometimes these depressions hold water and become lakes. Other times all that is left is a conical hole in the ground. The sinkholes are still active. On the eastern edge of Shoepac Lake, you can see collapses that occurred in 1937 and 1976.

Motor vehicles are prohibited in the 2,600 acres that make up the Sinkhole Area. The Sinkhole Pathway makes a wide loop around the area's five most dramatic holes. Observation decks at each sinkhole offer nice views and give you a real sense of the dramatic landscape. There are stairs at the first sinkhole for hikers inclined to make the 181-step trek to the bottom and back.

In 1939 a forest fire swept through this area, destroying nearly 40,000 acres. Along the pathway, you can still see evidence of this fire. The trail also passes through thick stands of aspens and jack pines, which have grown since the fire.

For more-adventurous hikers, especially those with a good map and compass, the Sinkhole Area is lined with fire lanes. The map at the trailhead has some of these marked out, but there are more to explore. The parking area and trailhead for the Sinkhole Pathway are just north of the Shoepac Lake State Forest Campground.

Another popular hike passes through the East Unit of the Tomahawk Creek Flooding campground: the 80-mile High Country Pathway, designed to offer backpackers a week of hiking in the wilderness. There is really no other trail like it in the Lower Peninsula. Other campgrounds on the pathway include Pigeon River (see page 105) and nearby Shoepac Lake. For day-hike purposes, the trail connects with the Sinkhole Pathway.

In recent years, mountain bikers have taken on the challenge of the High Country Pathway. The entire 80 miles represents sort of a marathon of mountain biking, and a careful cyclist can complete the loop in one day—usually by riding from sunup to a little after sundown. Considered an epic ride by the International Mountain Biking Association, this course requires that you be well prepared. You certainly don't want to find yourself 40 miles in with a mechanical problem and no backup plan.

Tomahawk Creek Flooding State Forest Campground

GETTING THERE

From Exit 282 off I-75 in Gaylord, drive 33 miles east on M-32. In Atlanta, turn left (north) onto M-33. In 15.5 miles, turn right onto Tomahawk Lake Highway; then, after 1 mile, turn right (south) onto Dam Road and follow the signs 0.8 mile to the campground.

GPS COORDINATES: N45° 12.784' W84° 11.099'

UPPER PENINSULA

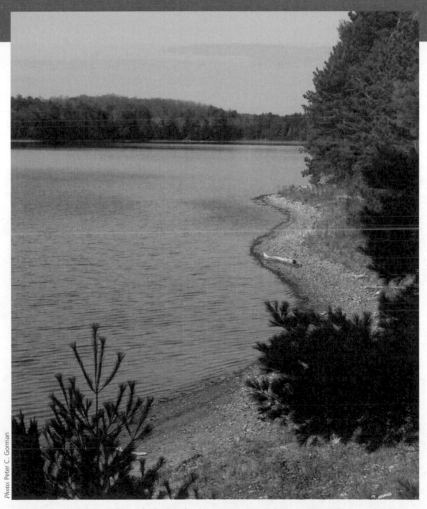

A view along the shoreline of Clark Lake (see Campground 49, page 163)

34

⛺ Bay View
National Forest Campground

Beauty ★★★★★ Privacy ★★★★ Spaciousness ★★★★★ Quiet ★★★★ Security ★★★★ Cleanliness ★★★★★

The sandy beach on Lake Superior attracts swimmers, sunbathers, and rock hunters.

Consider this: every year an average of 10,000 ships pass through the locks in Sault Ste. Marie, and that's only April–December, when the passage isn't closed due to ice. (A dramatic rise in the temperature of Lake Superior in recent years may mean that the locks will stay open longer in the future.) This number includes everything from Soo Locks tour boats to pleasure craft to the Great Lakes freighters (the workhorses of freshwater shipping). The freighters are the largest ships on the freshwater seas, and the largest of these are the thousand-footers that can carry more than 88,000 tons of cargo.

Recreationists have many great reasons to come to the Upper Peninsula—hunting and fishing, snowmobiling and dogsledding, fancy casinos, and some nice golf courses—but there is a certain pleasure in simply setting up a chair overlooking Lake Superior and watching the ships go by. From your campsite at Bay View Campground on the southern shore of Whitefish Bay, you can watch the biggest of these, the freighters (those sweet-water titans), make way for either the downlake passage toward Lake Huron or out into the open waters of Lake Superior.

The thick forest offers a shady, private respite from the rest of the world.

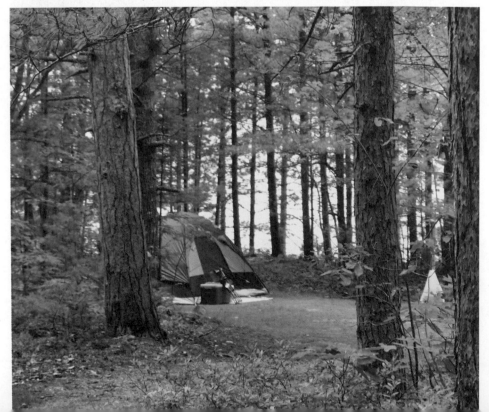

KEY INFORMATION

CONTACT: Hiawatha National Forest, Sault Ste. Marie Ranger District; 906-635-5311, tinyurl.com/bayviewcampground; reservations: 877-444-6777, recreation .gov/camping/campgrounds/234613

OPEN: Mid-May–early October

SITES: 26

EACH SITE HAS: Picnic table, fire pit with grill, and lantern post

ASSIGNMENT: First come, first served or by reservation

REGISTRATION: Self-register at campground

AMENITIES: Drinking water and vault toilets

PARKING: At sites

NIGHTLY FEE: $18

ELEVATION: 614'

RESTRICTIONS

PETS: On leash only

FIRES: Fire pits only

ALCOHOL: No stated restrictions; check ahead to confirm

VEHICLES: 2/site

OTHER: 8 people/site; 14-day stay limit

Located on West Lakeshore Drive (or Iroquois Road, depending on your map), the campground is part of the Whitefish Bay Scenic Byway. Sites worth visiting along the way include Point Iroquois Lighthouse to the east, the nearby Big Pine Day Use Area, and the Monocle Lake Campground and Recreation Area (covered on page 145).

Bay View has 26 sites. The layout is simple enough: the campground is essentially a long one-way pulloff from the main road. All but nine of the sites overlook Lake Superior from a low, wooded bluff. Down below, a sandy beach attracts swimmers, sunbathers, and rock hunters. Vault toilets (some quite new) and access to water from hand pumps are staggered throughout the length of the camp. There's hardly a place here where you'd find the facilities inconvenient, whether during the day or stumbling through the dark late at night.

The sites here can accommodate trailers and small RVs. Heavily wooded, with tall, thick pines and a mix of northern hardwoods, the hill down to the water is covered in lichens and ferns. Sites 25 and 26 are perhaps the best of the bunch. At the west end of the campground, a small parking area, just enough for several cars, marks the entrance to these spacious walk-in sites, which put tent campers as far from the vagaries of less courteous neighbors as is possible in a campground setting. Like the other sites, these are set up with a picnic table, fire pit, and lantern post. The lots are grassy, and a thinning of the trees allows for better views of the water.

In the summer, camp hosts occupy one of the sites. These folks are always good to have around and good to know. Often, hosts will return to the same campground year after year, giving the place some consistency. They carry with them the memories of past summers and are your best resource when it comes time to explore the area.

Along Lakeshore Drive, the road passes over numerous rivers and streams, all draining into the bay. Anglers catch lake trout and salmon near the bridges that span the flowing water. They also do well at nearby Monocle Lake. Ask the host about the best places to put in a boat or park for access to these flowing waters.

One mile east of Bay View, Hiawatha National Forest maintains the Big Pine Day Use Area, an excellent picnic spot that sits on a low sandy bluff, overlooking Lake Superior and a beautiful stretch of beach. The day-use area's most distinguishing feature is the stand of tall pines towering above, under which you will find a number of picnic tables liberally distributed. Check with the U.S. Forest Service about other public beaches along this part of the bay.

Bay View National Forest Campground

GETTING THERE

From Exit 386 off I-75, take M-28 West. After 7.5 miles, turn right (north) onto M-221 toward Brimley. In 2.5 miles, turn left (west) onto Iroquois Road/West Lakeshore Drive. After about 15 miles, the campground entrance will be on your right.

GPS COORDINATES: N46° 26.976' W84° 46.872'

35

⛺ Bewabic State Park Campground

Beauty ★★★★★ Privacy ★★★★★ Spaciousness ★★★★★ Quiet ★★★★ Security ★★★★★
Cleanliness ★★★★★

The terrain throughout the park is hilly and wooded, and the ground behind many sites falls away into a forest of pines and maples.

Crossing US 2 from Iron Mountain to Crystal Falls, dipping into Wisconsin along the way, you are passing through the Upper Peninsula's Menominee Range. Iron mining was a booming industry here not too long ago, and you see evidence of this everywhere you go in this part of the state. The Ojibwa word for "iron" was *pewabic*.

The presence of this metal in the Upper Peninsula was known for centuries, and throughout the Upper Peninsula you will find this word, and its many variations, tacked to a lot of different things—Pewabick Falls on the Little Iron River; the community of Pewabic on the Keweenaw Peninsula; and here, just north of the Wisconsin border, Bewabic State Park. (You find the same word spelled so many different ways because each person who came to learn the native languages wrote the sounds they heard differently. Bishop Frederic Baraga wrote *biwabic*, whereas early French explorers wrote it as *piouabic*.)

Bewabic State Park is 4 miles west of Crystal Falls, right off US 2. This 315-acre park features a large campground with modern and semimodern sites, tennis courts (a state park rarity), a beach and bathhouse on First Lake, and a short nature trail. Two sets of modern

A view of the beach and picnic area from an island in First Lake, just south of the campground

KEY INFORMATION

CONTACT: Michigan DNR–Bewabic State Park, 906-875-3324, michigan.gov/bewabic; reservations: 800-447-2757, midnrreservations.com

OPEN: Mid-May–October

SITES: 126 drive-up, 4 walk-in

EACH SITE HAS: Picnic table and fire pit; most have electricity

ASSIGNMENT: First come, first served or by reservation

REGISTRATION: At campground office

AMENITIES: Electricity, beach house with flushable toilets, bathhouse, and 4 vault toilets

PARKING: At sites and campground office

NIGHTLY FEE: $17 walk-in sites; $18–24 for others

ELEVATION: 1,407'

RESTRICTIONS

PETS: On leash only (maximum 6'); prohibited on beach

FIRES: Fire pits or grills only

ALCOHOL: Permitted

VEHICLES: Michigan Recreation Passport required (see page 8); 2 vehicles/site

OTHER: 6 people/site; 15-day stay limit

---

restrooms have running water and flush toilets, and the bathhouse in the day-use area has showers. Though fully prepared to host a troop of RVs, the campground is rather tent-friendly.

The 130 sites that make up the campground, which is well used throughout the season and is very shaded, are organized around three loops. The first loop, A, with sites 1–24 and 130, offers perhaps the best spots for tent camping in the park (I'll mention one notable exception later when looking at the third loop). The sites around this loop lie on the outside of the circle, facing in toward the wooded center. The terrain throughout the park is hilly and wooded, and the ground behind many sites falls away into a forest of pines and maples. Except for tent-only sites 17 and 18, the sites have electricity, but on the other hand, there are no pull-throughs and the dedicated bathroom facility is a pit toilet. The smattering of grass that covers the lots has a rough go of it, and campers are as likely to find a grassy spot as one of packed dirt on which to pitch a tent.

Sites 25–73 on the second loop, B, have decent lots against the loop's eastern side (one site, 43, is tent-only). Sites on the west side of the loop are close to the modern restrooms.

The third loop, C, with sites 74–129, has a strange mix of sites. Here, most of the lots come with electricity. Against the back are 11 pull-through sites. If RVs and fifth-wheels are to be found anywhere in the campground, it is here. That said, at the south end of the drive is a parking area for the park's four walk-in campsites (107–110). These are the exception I mentioned before. Decent buffers between sites throughout the campground provide ample privacy, but that doesn't compare with having your own spot in the woods. Located in a grove of tall maples, these walk-in sites each have a picnic table and fire pit, as well as a raised tent pad. The rolling forest floor makes this last item a necessity. The silence of the woods at these sites is broken only by the sound of the wind in the trees high above and the echo of twigs and sap falling on the blanket of last year's leaves below.

The state park is located on the northernmost of the Fortune Lakes. This chain of four lakes—aptly named First Lake, Second Lake, and so on—is popular with anglers who catch perch, walleye, pike, and bass. The lakes are connected by small channels and give paddlers some interesting water for exploring. First Lake also connects to Mud Lake, north of US 2.

First Lake is the largest of the bunch, and the park covers nearly the entire western shore, most of it undeveloped. The day-use area features a picnic shelter, a playground, tennis courts, a bathhouse, and a fine swimming beach. You will immediately notice the stone pavilion, which was built by the Civilian Conservation Corps in the 1930s. From the beach a trail heads east to a footbridge that leads to a small island.

Beyond the park, a number of sites highlight the region's mining history. Close by is Fortune Pond, just 0.5 mile north of US 2 on North Bristol Road, halfway between the park and Crystal Falls. The small lake here was once an open-pit iron mine that, in the 1950s, cranked out more than 1 million tons of iron ore. The county maintains a small park on the east side of the pond. The clear, deep water has attracted scuba divers by the score. At the end of the fishing pier, the bottom of the lake drops to 35 feet, and you can see all the way down. This is just one of the stops on the Iron County Heritage Trail (ironheritage.org), which connects historical sites from Crystal Falls to Iron River. To get a sense of the contribution iron mining has made to the region, be sure to stop at a few of these sites while you're in the area.

Bewabic State Park Campground

GETTING THERE

From downtown Crystal Falls, where US 2 and US 141 enter town from the south, follow US 2 for 4.5 miles west to the state park entrance, on your left.

GPS COORDINATES: N46° 05.658' W88° 25.524'

36

⛺ Big Knob State Forest Campground

Beauty ★★★★★ Privacy ★★★★ Spaciousness ★★★★ Quiet ★★★★ Security ★★★★★ Cleanliness ★★★★

This area is known for its dunes and swales, and lakeside sites access the beach by way of trails that lead out to the shore through low bushes and dune grass.

Big Knob Road is a narrow dirt path that wanders so much that you might be justified in questioning the sobriety of the surveyors who plotted it. As the arrow flies, Big Knob State Forest Campground at the road's end is a little more than 4 miles south. By car it's closer to 6. After you've spent hours of wading through the beginning-of-weekend summer traffic, leaving US 2 can be a jolt to the system. And when the road hasn't been recently graded, the drive offers plenty more jolts, this time of the variety that loosen the muffler and unseat carefully packed gear. But the campers who come here seeking solitude and a quiet stretch of beach know what they're about.

Located on the lake edge of a large swath of Lake Superior State Forest, the rustic campground here is one of the most ignored treasures on Lake Michigan. Twenty-three sites fill out the oddly B-shaped site map. Those closest to the water, sites 1–7, sit back from the shore a bit behind a low foredune. This area is known for its dunes and swales, and lakeside sites access the beach by way of trails that lead out to the shore through low bushes and dune grass, and over a boardwalk that crosses the low wet sections.

The campground affords easy access to the beach along Lake Michigan.

Photo: Theodore W./thedyrt.com

KEY INFORMATION

CONTACT: Tahquamenon Falls State Park, 906-293-3415, tinyurl.com/bigknob campground

OPEN: Year-round, though snow will prevent road access in winter

SITES: 23

EACH SITE HAS: Picnic table and fire pit

ASSIGNMENT: First come, first served; no reservations

REGISTRATION: Self-register at campground

AMENITIES: Hand-pumped potable water and vault toilets

PARKING: At sites

NIGHTLY FEE: $15

ELEVATION: 589'

RESTRICTIONS

PETS: On leash only

FIRES: Fire pits only

ALCOHOL: No stated restrictions; check ahead to confirm

VEHICLES: Michigan Recreation Passport required (see page 8); 2 vehicles/site

OTHER: 6 people/site; 15-day stay limit

Sites farther from the water sit in a forest made up primarily of pine. These are roomy spots with long gravel spurs that push the actual camping area back from the road. Water is available near the parking area from a hand pump, and the facilities include two outhouses—one for men, the other for women—at the far end of each loop. These are classic state forest toilets: narrow and tall, with translucent green plastic roofs (for light). They're cleaner than most, but they still have that airline-restroom feel, and there's always the worry that you might stumble and accidentally tip the things over.

The day-use area is used mostly by people who have come for the trails or for a low-key place for swimming. Anglers may stay and cast their lines on a few nearby inland lakes or even use the campground as a base camp for wider excursions. From the campground, you are close to a couple of trails that explore the local geography—in particular, the Big Knob–Crow Lake Foot Trails and the Marsh Lake Foot Trail. The 1.5-mile Marsh Lake hike leads through and around the lake and its attendant bogs. The trailhead begins at the parking area in the campground, heading out to the southwest.

The trailhead for Big Knob and Crow Lake is just off Big Knob Road, north of the campground a ways. (The trail is well posted.) The shortest hike takes you 0.3 mile up to the top of Big Knob itself. This short out-and-back is worthwhile for the view. On the other side of the street, the trail dives back into the woods for a 2.5-mile loop through old dunes and marsh, passing close to Crow Lake. The trail ends at a logging road that connects back to Big Knob Road.

These hikes put the area's unique ecology on display. You might see, for example, pitcher thistles, which make their home in the dunes around the upper Great Lakes. Dwarf lake irises are another rare find. These purple flowers with deep yellow accents are only found on the northern shores of Lakes Michigan and Huron. In 1998, this iris was named the official state wildflower. Another flower, Houghton's goldenrod, grows primarily around the straits area of northern Lakes Huron and Michigan.

The wetlands are a favorite with birds. Visitors often see ducks and terns, in addition to the ubiquitous seagulls, near the small dune ponds. Common loons are, um, common this far north, and campers who keep an eye on the sky may see bald eagles.

A bit farther afield, a nice out-and-back hike begins east of Scott Point and takes you west to Birch Point. The author of *Hiking Michigan's Upper Peninsula*, Eric Hansen, called this "arguably some of the most remote mainland shoreline on Lake Michigan." Hikers basically walk the shoreline, which includes dunes, rocky beach, long stretches of bedrock, and immense boulders. The hike begins at the Gould City Township Park at the southernmost end of Gould City Road. Following the lake west, the trek will take you about 2.5 miles to Birch Point. Interestingly, standing on the shore here, you're closer to Beaver Island than any other spot on Michigan's mainland.

Big Knob State Forest Campground

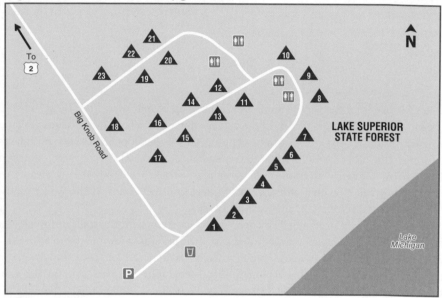

GETTING THERE

From Tuffy Street/Naubinway Road in Naubinway, drive west 7.6 miles on US 2, and turn left onto Big Knob Road. Drive south about 6 miles to the campground—you can't miss it.

GPS COORDINATES: N46° 02.340' W85° 35.634'

37

⛺ Black River Harbor National Forest Campground

Beauty ★★★★★ Privacy ★★★★ Spaciousness ★★★★★ Quiet ★★★★ Security ★★★★★ Cleanliness ★★★★★

Campers looking for a little recreation can use the North Country Trail as an out-and-back that will take them by all the significant falls on the Black River.

You will find scenic waterfalls throughout the Upper Peninsula. And while the eastern Upper Peninsula has Tahquamenon, Miners Falls, and perhaps Laughing Whitefish (the latter depending on where you draw the boundary between east and west), travelers making a waterfall tour don't really hit their stride until they get west of Marquette. With a decent waterfall map in hand, you'll pass close by some cataract or other, whatever route you take. There you have beauties, such as Black River Falls and Canyon Falls. Farther west are Bond Falls, north of Watersmeet, and Agate Falls, downriver from that, near M-28. An important route to add to any waterfall-viewing itinerary is the Black River Harbor Parkway (also known as Black River Road).

For 11 miles the road parallels the Black River, ending at Black River Harbor. In 1992, it was designated a National Forest Scenic Byway. The drive alone—winding and thickly wooded—would be worth the trip, but the real attractions along the byway are a series of five waterfalls and the day-use area at the journey's end.

It is here, right before the harbor, that the national forest has established the Black River Harbor Campground. Forty sites are situated on one large loop, tucked in between maple and birch trees. The camp offers water from a spigot and two sets of restrooms with flush toilets. The bathrooms can be found inside the loop at either end, quite set apart from the

Black River Harbor lies just east of its namesake campground.

CONTACT: Ottawa National Forest, Bessemer Ranger District; 906-932-1330, tinyurl.com/bigriverharbor; reservations: 877-444-6777, recreation.gov/camping /campgrounds/273343

OPEN: Late May–September

SITES: 40

EACH SITE HAS: Picnic table and fire pit

ASSIGNMENT: First come, first served or by reservation

REGISTRATION: Self-register at campground

AMENITIES: Pressurized water and toilets

PARKING: At sites

NIGHTLY FEE: $16

ELEVATION: 738'

RESTRICTIONS

PETS: On leash only

FIRES: Fire pits only

ALCOHOL: No stated restrictions; check ahead to confirm

VEHICLES: 2/site

OTHER: 8 people/site; 14-day stay limit

campsites. As you drive the paved road through the campground, you'll notice wide mowed paths, always on your left. Once inside the circle, all these pathways eventually lead to the toilets. There are no showers here.

Sites are spacious and grassy and come with a picnic table and fire pit. (There are more picnic tables overlooking Lake Superior and in the day-use area.) None of the campsites have views of Lake Superior, though at the northern end of camp, the Great Lake is visible just through the trees. A path leads down to the water and a wide, sandy beach.

This tends to be a busy campground throughout summer, so reservations are recommended. The next closest campground is to the east in the Porcupines Mountain Wilderness Area. Less than 5 miles away if you were to walk the shore of Lake Superior, Presque Isle Campground (see page 154) will take you more than an hour—38 miles, all told—to reach by car. Other nearby campgrounds include Little Girl's Point (operated by Gogebic County), which is northwest of Ironwood on the lake; the other rustic and modern campgrounds in the Porcupine Mountains; and the national forest facilities southeast of Ironwood.

Waterfall hunters should look out for four trailheads along the Black River Harbor Parkway. These paths lead to five waterfalls (from south to north): Great Conglomerate Falls, Potawatomi Falls, Gorge Falls, Sandstone Falls, and Rainbow Falls. Three other named falls are upstream: Narrows, Chippewa Falls, and Algonquin Falls. These are less impressive— Narrows doesn't even merit the word *Falls* in its name—and it's harder to get to.

Potawatomi Falls and Gorge Falls share a trailhead; if you have time for only one stop, make it this one. Potawatomi drops 30 feet in a gentle cascade. In low water, the falls divide around the large rock. The Gorge Falls downstream are no less impressive—dropping 25 feet through dark canyon walls.

One way to visit the falls is to hike awhile on the North Country Trail (NCT), which enters the area from the east, just south of Rainbow Falls. It follows the river north to the harbor and then doubles back on the west side of the river. The pathway leaves Lake Superior here, heading inland, and unless thru-hikers add the optional Superior Hiking Trail in northern Minnesota, they will not draw as close to the Great Lakes again. Campers looking for a little recreation can use the trail as an out-and-back that will take them by all the significant falls on the Black River.

The NCT crosses the Black River over a suspension bridge close to the harbor. On either side of the river's mouth, sandy beach stretches in both directions. The bridge gets you over the river to enjoy the eastern portion of the day-use area. Black River Harbor—one of only two harbors in the entire national forest system—offers restrooms, a small store selling concessions and supplies for boaters, and a nice place to picnic under the pines and hemlocks.

In late September and early October, the trees in this part of the country seem to catch on fire. Brilliant reds and oranges draw fall-color tourists from all over. One of the best views of this autumnal transformation can be found at the south end of the scenic byway at Copper Peak Ski Flying Hill, the only place in the western hemisphere where skiers can practice this extreme version of ski jumping. During the off-season, Copper Peak offers its Adventure Ride. First, the chairlift takes visitors 360 feet up to the top of Copper Peak (so named because copper is in the rocks). Then, an elevator takes them up another 18 stories (180 feet) to the top of the ski jump. On a good day, you can see Michigan, Wisconsin, Minnesota, and even Canada from this dizzying height. The views of the surrounding forest and Lake Superior are spectacular.

Black River Harbor National Forest Campground

GETTING THERE

From Moore Street in downtown Bessemer, drive 1.5 miles west on US 2 and turn right (north) onto Powderhorn Road/County Highway 511. In 3 miles, just past Big Powderhorn Mountain Resort, the road comes to a T at Black River Harbor Parkway/County Highway 513. Turn left and continue north 11.1 miles to the campground entrance, on your left. In case you miss it and have to turn around, CH 513 ends just 0.5 mile later at Lake Superior and Black River Harbor.

GPS COORDINATES: N46° 39.750' W90° 03.120'

38

⛺ Bond Falls Flowage Campground

Beauty ★★★★★ Privacy ★★★★★ Spaciousness ★★★★★ Quiet ★★★★★ Security ★★★★ Cleanliness ★★★★

Once you visit Bond Falls, just north of the flowage, you'll understand why so many people love this place.

There appears to always be some controversy circling the Bond Falls Flowage north of Watersmeet. The lake and most of the land around it belong to the Upper Peninsula Power Company (UPPCO). Public utilities are never very popular with nature lovers in the first place, and when a company owns a piece of property as picturesque and naturally beautiful as this, and its policies in turn affect one of the Upper Peninsula's most popular waterfalls and the quality of the river downstream, there's sure to be a concerned outcry over every decision. In recent years UPPCO sold off acreage around the lake for development, expanded the campground, and rebuilt the dam leading to Bond Falls. Each of these decisions has, at the very least, been cause for discussion.

Interestingly, the immense 2,100-acre lake that many seem anxious to protect from the power company was created by the power company. It is the result of a dam built on the Middle Branch of the Ontonagon River back in 1937. Water from the river and several feeder streams is captured in this reservoir and diverted by way of a flume to the South Branch of the Ontonagon River. The lake provides water to the Victoria Reservoir farther north, which requires a steady supply to power its generators. The flowage itself is a happy accident of the company's harnessing of the river to provide electricity to Copper Country.

Bond Falls is surrounded by wildflowers.

Photo: Craig Sterken/Shutterstock

KEY INFORMATION

CONTACT: Upper Peninsula Power Company, 906-827-3753

OPEN: June–September 15

SITES: 48

EACH SITE HAS: Picnic table, fire pit with grill, and lantern post

ASSIGNMENT: First come, first served; no reservations

REGISTRATION: At Bond Falls Outpost

AMENITIES: Hand-pumped water and vault toilets

PARKING: At sites

NIGHTLY FEE: $10

ELEVATION: 1,439'

RESTRICTIONS

PETS: On leash only

FIRES: In grills, fireplace, or fire pits only

ALCOHOL: No stated restrictions; check ahead to confirm

VEHICLES: 2 vehicles/site; 15-mph speed limit

OTHER: 4 people/site; 14-day stay limit; quiet hours 11 p.m.–6 a.m.

Once you visit Bond Falls, just north of the flowage, you'll understand why so many people love this place. It's a beautiful spot in the woods, and there is a lot to do and see. The region includes the Bond Falls Scenic Area, a day-use area on the north shore of the lake, and a fine campground of 48 sites spread out like a necklace around much of the lake. The campsites here can be divided into two groups. The first consists of the 20 sites found in the Bond Falls Consolidated Campground on the western shore of the lake. Located on a small point, paths to the west, north, and east lead to the water. Tucked into woods as they are, even this, the largest grouping of sites on the lake, offers a decent amount of privacy. There are several pull-through sites, and the facilities are accessible to folks using wheelchairs.

The dispersed sites around the flowage can be found along the west, north, and east shores. Bond Falls Road follows the lake around its west and north shores, and the campsites here are the easiest to get to. The choicest of the lot are those to the east—sites E1–E16. Sites E5–E7 sit at the base of a long point and face the setting sun, a nice feature anytime, but early and late in the season this means a longer evening in camp. Facilities throughout include vault toilets and water from hand pumps. Each site has a fire pit with grill and picnic table. Campers often bring their canoes and simply launch from the shore.

As spectacular as this lake is, most visitors come to Bond Falls to see the waterfall. Considered by many to be the most stunning falls in the Upper Peninsula, the river here tumbles 50 feet down a pyramid of boulders and rock. At its base, the water collects in a large pool before continuing south. A narrow trail leads up the rocks on the west side of the river, and you can get a great view this way. The state runs Bond Falls Scenic Area, and a Michigan Recreation Passport (see page 8) is required to park here. But come from camp or Bond Falls Road, and a nice trail leads to the upper side of the falls. Around its base a wide, somewhat ornate boardwalk keeps your feet dry and enables you to see the cascade from a number of perspectives.

Downstream, near M-28, the Ontonagon takes another tumble, this time a 40-foot drop down Agate Falls—certainly worth a visit. The water from Bond Falls to the confluence of the various Ontonagons north of here can be a little shallow, but upstream the Middle Branch can be navigated by canoe as far south as Watersmeet. From the bridge at US 45 to the flowage, you'll find more than 20 miles of good water. There are a few portages in there, so be sure to check out a decent river guide. The whole journey could take up to 10 hours, and a lot of folks choose to camp about halfway at Ottawa National Forest's Burneda Dam Campground.

Boat launches are located on both the north and south ends of the lake. And at the dam above the falls, kids will love stopping for some ice cream or other concessions at the Bond Falls Outpost. The store also sells souvenirs and some camp supplies.

Bond Falls Flowage Campground

GETTING THERE

From First Street/Old US 2 in Watersmeet, drive north on US 45 for 9.6 miles, and turn right (east) onto Bond Falls Road. In 3.3 miles, look for the Bond Falls Outpost on your right; here you can pick up a map of the campground and register.

GPS COORDINATES: N46° 24.492' W89° 07.800'

39

Brevoort Lake
National Forest Campground

Beauty ★★★★★ Privacy ★★★★ Spaciousness ★★★★★ Quiet ★★★★★ Security ★★★★★
Cleanliness ★★★★★

Brevoort Lake is known for its fishing and is considered by many to be one of the state's finest fishing lakes.

From the bridge to Naubinway, US 2 follows the gentle northwesterly curve of Lake Michigan. At first the route's main attractions are the Weird Michigan Wax Museum; the curiously enduring Mystery Spot; and numerous places selling sandwiches, exotic jerky, and views of the straits. The bridge serves as a gateway, and businesses do a brisk trade welcoming travelers to the Upper Peninsula and offering folks on their way home a last chance at vacation memories.

The commercial strip doesn't last, however, and soon passengers on westbound US 2 look out their windows to see miles of sandy Lake Michigan beach. Each summer, thousands of visitors get no farther into the Upper Peninsula than this. They find a place to hole up at night and spend their days soaking up the sun.

And there are certainly a lot of places to stay. Hotels and motels in St. Ignace are just 30 minutes away, of course, but the Hiawatha National Forest and Lake Superior State Forest maintain a mess of campgrounds, all close by. The most popular has to be the national forest's Brevoort Lake Campground. Located on a small point that separates Boedne Bay from the rest of this stunning inland lake, the unit offers 70 sites. Most are available on a

The campground at Brevoort Lake is popular with families.

KEY INFORMATION

CONTACT: Hiawatha National Forest, St. Ignace Ranger District; 906-643-7900, tinyurl.com/brevoortlake; reservations: 877-444-6777, recreation.gov/camping /campgrounds/234080

OPEN: Early May–early October

SITES: 70

EACH SITE HAS: Picnic table, fire pit with grill, and lantern post

ASSIGNMENT: First come, first served or by reservation

REGISTRATION: Self-register at campground

AMENITIES: Pressurized drinking water from a spigot, wheelchair-accessible restrooms

PARKING: At sites

NIGHTLY FEE: $20 single sites, $40 double sites

ELEVATION: 630'

RESTRICTIONS

PETS: On leash only

FIRES: Fire pits only

ALCOHOL: No stated restrictions; check ahead to confirm

VEHICLES: 2/site

OTHER: 8 people/site; 14-day stay limit

first-come, first-served basis, but the campground does set aside a small number that can be reserved. This close to Lake Michigan and the bridge, the campground stays busy throughout the summer. But if you can't find a site here, you can always try Little Brevoort, which is the state forest campground next door, or any one of the public campgrounds along US 2, including the Foley Creek National Forest Campground north of St. Ignace and the Straits State Park—all decent options.

The first 49 sites on Brevoort Lake thread their way up and around the spit of land that inserts itself between Boedne Bay and the lake. The remaining 21 sites can be found along the south shore of the bay. Most of the sites here, 39 all tallied, are on the water, and only a dozen on the peninsula lie on the inside of the loop. The property is wooded throughout, and each site comes prepped for campers with a wooden picnic table, a fire pit with an iron grill, and a lantern post. Flush toilets and drinking water can be found in convenient locations throughout the camp.

Next to the day-use area, a camp store sells groceries and other necessities, including fishing gear. It also rents boats and canoes. Anglers will find the staff helpful. Brevoort Lake is known for its fishing and is considered by many to be one of the state's finest fishing lakes. At 4,233 acres, the lake is large and also shallow, 10–30 feet deep. Anglers can hunt the day away—looking for the best spot—without bumping into each other. Walleye are prime targets for the casters who troll the lake (the U.S. Forest Service built a large walleye-spawning reef here years back), but folks also pull in smallmouth bass, perch, panfish, and northern pike.

The campground doesn't offer much in the way of hiking. The 0.5-mile Ridge Interpretive Trail leads walkers up a dune and has views of Lake Michigan, and it takes all of 20 minutes to complete. Driving into the camp, you may notice a trail crossing the road that offers the promise of serious hiking. The North Country Trail (NCT) crosses east–west here before turning north toward Tahquamenon. The NCT is no day hike and comes with no convenient way to loop back home, but hikers might enjoy doing an out-and-back on a portion of this cross-country trail.

For swimming, the sandy beach that borders the eastern shore of the peninsula can be a happy alternative to the Great Lake—the waters of Lake Michigan are slow to warm in summer, but inland lakes are quicker to grab hold of and hold on to the heat. That said, the nearby stretch of Lake Michigan is beautiful, especially when enjoyed from the dunes that separate the larger lake from Brevoort Lake. In the summer, cars line up, parked alongside US 2. Yet the beach is never crowded and always has room for sunbathers to spread out.

Farther west along the highway, you come to the mouth of the Cut River. The water flows down a tall gorge. If you're not paying attention, you may not even notice that the ground has continued to rise above lake level. By the time you cross the Cut River Bridge, the idea of a river flowing 147 feet below seems a little odd. Picnic areas at both ends of the bridge allow you to get out of the car, stretch your legs, and explore this interesting structure. Then start the descent. Staircases on either side take you down to the water. Trails follow the river and lead you out to another beautiful beach on Lake Michigan.

For more wilderness and a chance at some river fishing, the South Branch of the Carp River flows west to east and through the Mackinac Wilderness, which is just a few miles north of Brevoort Lake. The wetlands bordering the river comprise much of this 12,000-acre preserve. With no roads and no footpaths, most visitors experience the wilderness only by paddling in on the Carp River or as they travel the St. Ignace–Trout Lake Rail Trail, which runs alongside M-123.

Brevoort Lake National Forest Campground

GETTING THERE

From the Mackinac Bridge, take the second exit off I-75 North (Exit 344B), and follow US 2 West almost exactly 17 miles to Forest Service Road 3108, where you'll see a sign for the campground. Turn right (north) and follow the road 1.2 miles to the campground entrance.

GPS COORDINATES: N46° 00.582' W84° 58.278'

40

Carney Lake State Forest Campground

Beauty ★★★★ Privacy ★★★★ Spaciousness ★★★★★ Quiet ★★★★★ Security ★★★★★ Cleanliness ★★★★

Rather than distracting from the scenery, the cabins give the place the feel of an old North Woods hunting and fishing camp.

As you head west across the Upper Peninsula, Dickinson County is the first you come to that doesn't touch either Lake Michigan or Lake Superior. Only two counties in the Upper Peninsula can be called landlocked, and the other is Dickinson's neighbor to the west, Iron County. Here, the boundaries are defined not by the glacial basins of the Great Lakes but by the meandering paths of the Brule and Menominee Rivers. US 2, the main east–west highway, cuts across from Escanaba, turning northwest in Iron Mountain, and continues into Wisconsin for a spell before reaching Crystal Falls and eventually Ironwood.

Northeast of Iron Mountain—far from where the Porcupine Mountains overlook the cold gray of Lake Superior and hours from the sandy dune beaches of Lake Michigan—you will find a really nice place to camp, though it takes some driving. First, you drive north to Merriman and then head east along U.S. Forest Service roads. Six miles of gravel roller coaster later, Carney Lake waits in a forest of white pines and birches. You will find the campground at the northwest corner of the lake.

Carney Lake State Forest Campground consists of a simple loop of 16 grassy campsites. You can't make reservations here, so you obviously can't always count on getting the exact site you want, but the campground sees light use throughout the summer, and a happy alternative site is almost always available. Six sites along the lake have trails leading down

Wake up to foggy mornings on Carney Lake.

KEY INFORMATION

CONTACT: Michigan DNR–Bewabic
 State Park, 906-875-3324, tinyurl.com
 /carneylake

OPEN: November–April

SITES: 16

EACH SITE HAS: Picnic table and fire pit

ASSIGNMENT: First come, first served;
 no reservations

REGISTRATION: Self-register at campground

AMENITIES: Hand-pumped potable water
 and vault toilets

PARKING: At sites

NIGHTLY FEE: $15

ELEVATION: 1,129'

RESTRICTIONS

PETS: On leash only

FIRES: Fire pits only

ALCOHOL: No stated restrictions; check
 ahead to confirm

VEHICLES: Michigan Recreation Passport
 required (see page 8); 2 vehicles/site

OTHER: 6 people/site; 15-day stay limit

to the water. Site 9 sits on a rise with a great view of Carney Lake. More graveled and open than the rest, this site, I imagine, is popular for campers towing a small trailer. The facilities are limited to vault toilets and water from a hand pump.

Carney Lake itself is a gem. Surrounded by woods, a few cabins on the far shore are set back into the trees. Rather than distracting from the scenery, they add to it, giving the place that feel of an old North Woods hunting and fishing camp. The lake reaches 30 feet deep out in front of the campground, and the southwest half of the lake is a much shallower 10–20 feet. All told, its surface area spreads out over 117 acres.

Bring your boat and cast a line for smallmouth bass, walleye, northern pike, pumpkin-seed, and sunfish. The lake drains to the north, and at both ends you will find marsh and swampland. Rocks and gravel, however, line both the campground side of the lake and the opposite shore.

Part of the campground's appeal is how little else there is to do here but camp (and perhaps fish). For more recreational-type activities, consider a trip south to the 1,800-acre Fumee Lake Natural Area, due east of Iron Mountain; to reach it, you'll have to drive back through town and access the park from US 2. Four main trails offer everything from easygoing 1.5-mile hikes to strenuous 4.4-mile loops. An additional 4.5 miles of rugged singletrack are open to hikers, mountain bikers, and, in the winter, cross-country skiers. The centerpiece of the preserve is the 507-acre Fumee Lake, which, combined with neighboring Little Fumee, offers 5 miles of undeveloped shoreline. The area is used by educators to teach ecology and is home to common loons, bald eagles, and 17 different species of orchids.

At some point, stop by **Damian's Pasta Works** in Iron Mountain for some of the best Italian food in the state (909 S. Stephenson Ave.; 906-774-3058). European immigrants poured into the Upper Peninsula in the 19th century, looking for work in the mines. Throughout the UP, communities still reflect the influence of their old-world forebears, many of whom came from such places as Norway, Finland, Italy, and England and usually settled in enclaves with their own people. The Italian restaurants here are legendary. Damian's does away with the usual amenities (such as tables and chairs) and best suits the camping ethos. The menu has the usual Italian fare with some local additions. Order from the counter and take away boxes of linguine, fettuccine, or good old spaghetti with one of their eight sauces.

They also have pasties (meat-and-potato-filled turnovers brought over from Cornwall in southwest England) and excellent sandwiches.

Carney Lake State Forest Campground

GETTING THERE

From US 2 just north of Iron Mountain, bear right at the Y onto M-95. In about 4 miles, you'll come to the tiny community of Merriman—no more than a couple of shops on the corner, all of which looked out of business during my last visit—and turn right (east) onto Sportsmens Club Road. After 2.6 miles, come to a T at Carney Lake Road and turn right; in another 0.6 mile, turn left at the fork to remain on Carney Lake Road, and follow it about 3.5 miles east and then south to the campground on the lake.

GPS COORDINATES: N45° 53.526' W87° 56.496'

41

⛺ Courtney Lake National Forest Campground

Beauty ★★★★ Privacy ★★★★ Spaciousness ★★★★ Quiet ★★★★★ Security ★★★★★ Cleanliness ★★★★★

A small inlet off Courtney Lake creates a point on which the two best sites in camp can be found.

This close to the Keweenaw Peninsula, you've officially entered the Upper Peninsula's Copper Country. The history of copper runs deep in this part of the world. The first explorers came here and heard of copper boulders too big for a man to carry. By that time, American Indians had been pulling the pliable metal out of the ground for 7,000 years. It was widely traded—archaeologists have found artifacts of Keweenaw copper throughout North America.

While most of the commercial mining during the 19th and 20th centuries took place on the peninsula proper, which is where you will find the Copper Country Trail National Scenic Byway, such towns as nearby Mass City and Greenland once thrived on copper. Mass City mainly attracted immigrants from Finland—families who came a long way to eke a living out of the ground, both mining and farming where they could. Some reminders of the town's heyday remain, although you'll see a lot of that gentle decay found in old mining towns all over the country.

Despite this area's commercial history, you can easily escape the hustle and bustle of urban life here.

KEY INFORMATION

CONTACT: Ottawa National Forest, Ontonagon Ranger District; 906-884-2411, tinyurl.com/courtneylake

OPEN: Late May–September

SITES: 21 (14 overlook the lake)

EACH SITE HAS: Picnic table, fire pit, and lantern post

ASSIGNMENT: First come, first served; no reservations

REGISTRATION: Self-register at campground

AMENITIES: Pressurized water faucets and vault toilets

PARKING: At sites

NIGHTLY FEE: $14

ELEVATION: 885'

RESTRICTIONS

PETS: On leash only

FIRES: Fire pits only

ALCOHOL: No stated restrictions; check ahead to confirm

VEHICLES: 2/site

OTHER: 8 people/site; 14-day stay limit

Courtney Lake is about 8 miles east of Greenland and Mass City in the Ottawa National Forest. Located on this 33-acre lake is a small campground of 21 sites. On a low bluff covered in hardwoods, the campground wraps around the southwest corner of the lake, with beautifully situated sites overlooking the water. Each site has a short packed-gravel spur for parking and a grassy lot for pitching a tent. And, in true national forest fashion, each is outfitted with a picnic table, fire pit with an iron grill, and lantern post. Other facilities include vault toilets and water from a pressurized faucet.

There's hardly an undesirable site to be found in the campground. Site 20 is particularly nice, as are 9 and 10. Site 9 offers less room than its neighbors but has a great view of the water. Site 10 sits back from the road, folded into a grove of surrounding pines. A small inlet off Courtney Lake creates a point on which the two best sites in camp can be found. Sites 15 and 16 are both walk-in sites, offering the most privacy and best access to the water. A sign designates these as being reserved for tent camping only—a message that seems a little unnecessary given the posts blocking vehicles and trailers from progressing past the parking area.

Around camp, activities include boating and fishing on Courtney Lake, or swimming at the day-use area's small beach. A short 2.2-mile hike through the woods, complete with signage to annotate the trip, begins at a trailhead south of site 7. Called the Circle of Life Interpretive Trail, it includes a boardwalk platform for viewing a bog. Also nearby: the Old Grade Ski Trail. This old railroad grade, from a time when locomotives pulled lumber across the Upper Peninsula, has been repurposed as a cross-country-skiing trail. A nearly 2-mile path connects the campground to the main trail, which in turn offers 4.5 miles of skiing through the national forest. The path is groomed weekly during the season. Be aware, however, that the powers that be do not maintain the campground in the winter, so any snow that falls will remain until spring.

Beyond Courtney Lake but not too far from the campground, the town of Greenland offers some short hikes with stunning views. On the hill above Greenland, you simply park at the Ontonagon County Fairgrounds. From there, a steep path continues up the hill. The first view you get is a look toward the northwest, extending all the way to Lake Superior. A little later on, the view to the southeast opens, and you can see the forest spreading out to Mass City and beyond.

For a taste of the area's copper-mining history and a diversion from the restful day-to-day of camp, visit the **Adventure Mining Company** in Greenland (200 Adventure Ave.; 906-883-3371, adventureminetours.com). With hardhats and headlamps, visitors are led into the dark Adventure Mine to learn firsthand what it was like to work here. Though the mine was active for 70 years, beginning in 1850, you can still see copper in the walls. Bring a coat—it's chilly underground year-round. If the idea of the mine tour leaves you feeling claustrophobic, they also have aboveground tours and a decent gift shop.

Finally, if your return trip takes you east along M-38, pick up one of the legendary giant cinnamon rolls at the **Hilltop Restaurant,** 5 miles south of Baraga on US 41 in L'Anse (906-524-7858, sweetroll.com). These huge, gooey delights will leave you sticky and wanting more all the way home.

Courtney Lake National Forest Campground

GETTING THERE

From US 41 in Baraga, head west on M-38. After about 22 miles, turn left (south) onto Courtney Lake Road. There's good signage all the way from M-38 a mile south to the campground.

GPS COORDINATES: N46° 45.096' W88° 56.436'

42

⚠ Henry Lake National Forest Campground

Beauty ★★★★ Privacy ★★★★★ Spaciousness ★★★★★ Quiet ★★★★★ Security ★★★★★
Cleanliness ★★★★★

Carved out of a mix of hardwoods and pines, the campsites are spacious and grassy, and many are edged in thick ferns.

You will find four campgrounds in this book from the western Upper Peninsula's Gogebic County, twice what any other county in the UP can boast. Henry Lake is probably the humblest of the bunch. Both Black River Harbor and the Presque Isle Campground in the Porcupine Mountains State Wilderness front Lake Superior. Clark Lake serves as a doorway to the legendary Sylvania Wilderness. Henry Lake, on the other hand, offers 11 quiet sites on a small lake. The farthest west of a series of national forest campgrounds that lie between US 2 and the Wisconsin border, Henry Lake is representative of the region's camping. Neighboring campgrounds include Moosehead Lake, Pomeroy Lake, Bobcat Lake, and Langford Lake.

The pattern you notice here tells a lot about the local geography: There are many lakes just south of US 2 once you get west of Watersmeet. If you expand the region to include the area south into Wisconsin, you will find country overflowing with hundreds of lakes. You also find an important watershed. Most of the lakes on the Michigan side of the border flow into Lake Superior. Those south make their way to the Mississippi. (It's not until you get a bit farther east that the lakes and streams of northern Wisconsin begin to flow toward Lake Michigan.)

Placid Henry Lake is ideal for paddling.

KEY INFORMATION

CONTACT: Ottawa National Forest, Bessemer Ranger District; 906-932-1330, tinyurl.com /henrylakecampground

OPEN: Late-May–late-September

SITES: 11

EACH SITE HAS: Picnic table and fire pit

ASSIGNMENT: First come, first served; no reservations

REGISTRATION: At the entrance pay station

AMENITIES: Hand-pumped water and vault toilets

PARKING: At sites

NIGHTLY FEE: $13

ELEVATION: 1,592'

RESTRICTIONS

PETS: On leash only

FIRES: Fire pits only

ALCOHOL: No stated restrictions; check ahead to confirm

VEHICLES: 2/site

OTHER: 8 people/site; 14-day stay limit

In the heart of a national forest, lakes and rivers, and camping facilities, you find 43-acre Henry Lake and its truly hospitable campground. Eleven grassy sites line up along the north shore of the lake. Most are too far back for a view of the water, but three of them—sites 5, 7, and 9—let you see the lake from camp. Carved out of a mix of hardwoods and pines, the campsites are spacious and grassy, and many are edged in thick ferns. The sites themselves are set far back from the road and offer all the privacy in the world.

Two vault toilets near the campground entrance and one at the boat launch, as well as water from a hand pump, complete the camp's list of luxuries. A boat launch and a fishing pier round out the facilities. Located this far north and quite a drive from the closest town, the campground feels safe, even without a host camper overseeing the property.

Henry Lake is relatively shallow, only 30 feet deep at the middle. Fish attractors at the fishing pier and directly across the lake from the pier provide habitat and help support the fishery of largemouth bass, bluegills, perch, and pumpkinseed (a sunfish so named for its unique coloring). The lake has a wide gravel boat ramp, and the pier east of the ramp is accessible by wheelchair. A nice packed-gravel trail leads from the parking area out to the dock.

The West Branch of the Presque Isle River flows close to Lake Henry. The upper portions of the Presque Isle offer easy paddling, suitable for newbies. Farther downstream, however, the Presque Isle serves up some of the most dangerous, yet at times still doable, whitewater in the state. For the easy stretch of river, put in at the Teal canoe landing north of Henry Lake on Forest Service Road 8100. This puts you on the West Branch of the river. The trip will take you through the Presque Isle River Flooding and north of US 2. At one point, there's a long portage around Yondata Falls. After that, the river continues at a leisurely pace to M-28. Canoeing or kayaking north of M-28 is for experts, and even they sometimes balk at the challenge.

Taking advantage of miles of U.S. Forest Service roads, the Pomeroy/Henry Lake Mountain Bike Complex offers mountain bikers 100 miles of loops through the national forest and around numerous lakes. This isn't the kind of mountain biking that sends you flying through the woods down steep singletrack, braking and leaning hard into the turns, or hopping over downed logs; rather, this is a place where the whole family can ride together. You don't really even need a mountain bike to tackle these loops, which have an easy grade and

Explore hundreds of miles of trails on a hybrid or mountain bike.

moderate hills, though folks with thin-tired road bikes will run into some trouble. To get a map of all the loops, stop by the Western Upper Peninsula Convention & Visitor Bureau in Ironwood, or give them a call at 906-932-4850.

Henry Lake National Forest Campground

GETTING THERE

From US 2, follow M-64 South into and through the town of Marenisco for 5.6 miles; then turn right (west) onto FS 8100. The campground is 4.6 miles ahead on your right, just northwest of Henry Lake.

GPS COORDINATES: N46° 19.824' W89° 47.556'

43

Monocle Lake National Forest Campground

Beauty ★★★★★ Privacy ★★★★ Spaciousness ★★★★ Quiet ★★★★★ Security ★★★★★ Cleanliness ★★★★★

From the bluff you can see Canada in the distance and Whitefish Bay, as well as ships entering and leaving the St. Mary's River.

A 20-mile stretch of West Lakeshore Drive (also known as Iroquois Road), a route beginning just west of Brimley that ends at M-123, has been designated as the Whitefish Bay Scenic Byway. It's noted particularly for various recreational opportunities and sites of historical importance: a typical itinerary might include stopping at Brimley State Park, fishing or kayaking in Whitefish Bay, visiting the Bay Mills Reservation, touring the Point Iroquois Lighthouse, and camping next to Monocle Lake.

Between Bay Mills and Point Iroquois on Lake Superior's Whitefish Bay, you'll find two small inland lakes. The southernmost of the pair is a smallish body of water nearly bisected by a thin point, the aptly named Spectacle Lake. A short ways to the northwest is its neighbor, the oblong Monocle Lake. Behind the lakes, running parallel with the shore of the bay, a tall ridge rises from the forest, creating a scenic backdrop.

The sandy shoreline of Monocle Lake is a great spot for a picnic.

KEY INFORMATION

CONTACT: Hiawatha National Forest, Sault Ste. Marie Ranger District; 906-635-5311, tinyurl.com/monoclelake; reservations: 877-444-6777, recreation.gov/camping/campgrounds/234617

OPEN: Late-May–late September

SITES: 42

EACH SITE HAS: Picnic table, fire pit, and lantern post

ASSIGNMENT: Online or by phone

REGISTRATION: Self-register at campground

AMENITIES: Pressurized water and vault toilets

PARKING: At sites

NIGHTLY FEE: $18

ELEVATION: 652'

RESTRICTIONS

PETS: On leash only

FIRES: Fire pits only

ALCOHOL: No stated restrictions; check ahead to confirm

VEHICLES: 2/site

OTHER: 8 people/site; 14-day stay limit

The campground on Monocle Lake is part of the Hiawatha National Forest. Most of the sites are nestled in a sprawling stand of tall maples. Other trees include aspens and white birches. The road through the camp is paved, and most sites are floored in packed dirt. None of the sites front the lake, though a few—sites 29 and 30, for example—sit directly across the road from the water and offer nice views. I also liked sites 13–16. These are found on the forest side of the campground, surrounded by maples, with plenty of privacy. Facilities include drinking water and vault toilets but no showers.

The day-use part of the facility includes a picnic area, a boat launch, a swimming beach, and a decent little nature hike. The lake is the big attraction. At 172 acres, this respectable lake counters its size with surprising depth (up to 55 feet) and great scenery. Private property makes up its north end, but all along its western shore is that impressive ridge I mentioned before. Its south end features a sandy beach, offering a somewhat warmer alternative to a dip in Lake Superior. Anglers casting a line here—from a boat or the park's fishing pier—pull in northern pike, smallmouth bass, and yellow perch. The Michigan Department of Natural Resources watches the walleye population closely and stocks the lake with the fish in hopes of creating a sustainable population.

The Monocle Lake Loop Trail leads hikers through 2 miles of a northern hardwood forest. The trail begins as a level path, accessible to visitors using wheelchairs. As the trail crosses wetlands, a boardwalk keeps your feet dry. A beaver dam along the way would be of special interest to kids, and you might also see blue herons by the water and ospreys diving toward the lake for fish. After about 0.25 mile, the trail leads up to a scenic overlook. This is where the sweet innocence of this stroll through the woods takes a serious turn. It's a steep, strenuous climb to the top, but, from the bluff, you will be able to see Canada in the distance and Whitefish Bay, as well as ships entering and leaving the St. Mary's River. This stunning view makes the climb worthwhile.

Beyond the campground, be sure to take in some of the historical sites. Just up the road, the Point Iroquois Lighthouse guides ships entering the St. Mary's River. The point is named for an event that took place here in the late 1600s. The Iroquois people hold a significant place in the history of upstate New York and in the colonial wars in America and Canada. Though their influence extends farther east in Canada and on Lake Ontario, the Iroquois name is not bandied about much in Michigan. Back in 1662, as the Iroquois were looking to expand their territory into the Great Lakes, they sent a war party west to the shores of Whitefish Bay. The Ojibwa living in this region discovered that the group was camped on this point and attacked. The Iroquois were wiped out after a day of fighting, and this battle became the last in a series that ended the Iroquois's ambitions for this territory.

About 200 years later, a lighthouse was erected on the point. When you visit today, you see the lighthouse and residence that were built in 1870 to replace the original tower. A visit to the lighthouse should include taking some time to stroll through the maritime museum there, which is maintained by the Bay Mills–Brimley Historical Research Society.

Monocle Lake National Forest Campground

GETTING THERE

From Exit 386 off I-75, take M-28 West. After 7.5 miles, turn right (north) onto M-221 toward Brimley. In 2.5 miles, turn left (west) onto Iroquois Road/West Lakeshore Drive. Then, in 6.2 miles, turn left at the campground sign onto West Park Road, and follow it 0.9 mile to the campground.

GPS COORDINATES: N46° 28.224' W84° 38.358'

44

⛺ Petes Lake
National Forest Campground

Beauty ★★★★★ Privacy ★★★★★ Spaciousness ★★★★★ Quiet ★★★★★ Security ★★★★★
Cleanliness ★★★★★

This campground is embraced by a forest of dark green throughout the summer.

The Hiawatha National Forest divides nicely into two units. The eastern portion of the forest stretches from Whitefish Bay down to the Straits of Mackinac. The western portion begins at the western edge of Pictured Rocks National Lakeshore, reaching halfway between Munising and Marquette. Its southern edge is along Lake Michigan, including the shores of Big and Little Bays de Noc and the peninsula between them. Combined, both halves total nearly 900,000 acres of forest.

Petes Lake Campground falls roughly in the center of the western unit. This part of the forest is known for dozens of small inland lakes and the Sturgeon and Indian Rivers. The area is a sportsman's paradise, and Petes Lake offers some of its best camping. Located just 13 miles south of Munising and 25 miles north of US 2 (a few miles west of where it passes through Manistique), the campground is convenient to the Upper Peninsula's major travel

The pier at Petes Lake is a good place to cast a line or just relax and take in the views.

Photo: Oleksandr Koretsky/Shutterstock

KEY INFORMATION

CONTACT: Hiawatha National Forest, Munising Ranger District; 906-387-2512, tinyurl.com/peteslake; reservations: 877-444-6777, recreation.gov/camping/campgrounds/233174

OPEN: Mid-May–late September

SITES: 43 standard sites (2 are tent-only), plus 5 group sites

EACH SITE HAS: Picnic table, fire pit with grill, and lantern post

ASSIGNMENT: Online or by phone

REGISTRATION: Self-register at campground

AMENITIES: Drinking water and vault toilets

PARKING: At sites

NIGHTLY FEE: $20 tent-only sites, $22 for tent/RV sites, $40 for group sites

ELEVATION: 809'

RESTRICTIONS

PETS: On leash only

FIRES: Fire pits only

ALCOHOL: No stated restrictions; check ahead to confirm

VEHICLES: 2/site

OTHER: 8 or 16 people/site; 14-day stay limit

---

routes. Yet the main road through here, H-13, is hardly a busy thoroughfare. Most traffic north and south follows M-94, and this contributes to the campground's remote feel.

Forty-eight campsites, laid out in a shape that resembles a split hot-dog bun, sit on the northern shore of Petes Lake, less than a mile east of H-13. The road through the camp is paved, and the individual sites have gravel spurs.

The surrounding woods lend sites plenty of privacy. This campground is embraced by a forest of dark green throughout the summer. The two walk-in sites, 7A and 8A, make Petes Lake especially attractive. You will find parking for these sites next to the trailhead on the eastern edge of camp. The first is a short ways through the woods. Site 7A is a spacious lawn overlooking Petes Lake. Offering little in the way of shade, the lot makes up for it with enough room for a private game of Ultimate Frisbee. The second site, located 0.25 mile east, also offers a view of the lake. A stand of tall pines gives the spot the feel of a rustic hideaway.

The trail out to the sites serves another purpose as well. It is mainly used by hikers and bikers as part of the Bruno's Run Trail, a 9-mile path that connects Petes Lake with a string of neighboring lakes. Bruno's Run attracts hikers and snowshoers but is also the only single-track mountain-biking trail in the county. Backpackers making a multiday trip can stay at Petes Lake or Widewaters Campground, or set up on Ewing Point. The latter spot is one of the national forest's dispersed campgrounds. The one walk-in site there features a pit toilet but no drinking water. Another option, and one that would allow you to carry less gear, would be to rent the cabin on McKeever Lake.

East of H-13, the trail winds around several lakes: Petes, McKeever, Wedge, and Dipper. Crossing to the west of H-13, the path follows the Indian River to Widewaters Campground. Leaving the river and heading north to Moccasin Lake, the trail leads through the Hemlock Cathedral—a stand of hemlocks more than a century old. From Moccasin Lake, the trail turns east back to Petes Lake. Along the way hikers walk over rolling terrain, through marsh, and across many a stream.

Mountain bikers will find the route an easy afternoon's ride. Not as technical as some of the trails you might find up near Marquette, the path still offers more challenges than people used to riding local dirt roads will be accustomed to. There are some great places to stop and rest and take in the view along the way.

Anglers, of course, will know all about the local lakes. There are quite a few, and boat access is easy to come by. In addition to the still waters, there is also the Indian River. Paddlers and anglers alike will find Petes Lake a convenient point for accessing the river. The Widewaters Campground on Fish Lake is a fine put-in. Downstream from there you can float 36 miles of river to Indian Lake, which is northwest of Manistique—that's well over 20 hours of canoeing. (Also feeding the Indian River is Kitch-iti-kipi, meaning "big spring." At Palms Book State Park, you can take the observation raft out over the spring and look down through 40 feet of crystal-clear water.) With primitive campgrounds conveniently spaced along the route, the river would perhaps be better suited for a wilderness paddling trip.

Petes Lake National Forest Campground

GETTING THERE

Leave I-75 at Exit 352, heading west and then north on M-123. After a little more than 33 miles, turn left (west) onto M-28 toward Newberry. Drive 78.5 miles and, just as you enter Wetmore, turn left (south) onto Connors Road/H-13. After about 10 miles, you'll see the sign for Petes Lake on the left, on Forest Service Road 2173. (If you come to the sign for Widewaters Campground, you've gone too far south.) Follow FS 2173 for 0.5 mile; then turn right (south) and arrive at the campground in another 0.5 mile.

GPS COORDINATES: N46° 13.752' W86° 35.958'

Pictured Rocks National Lakeshore:
TWELVEMILE BEACH CAMPGROUND

Beauty ★★★★★ Privacy ★★★★★ Spaciousness ★★★★★ Quiet ★★★★★ Security ★★★★★
Cleanliness ★★★★★

If you're going to hoof it all the way to the Pictured Rocks, a view of Lake Superior should not be missed.

The Upper Peninsula is bounded to the north by the lake the French called *le lac supérieur.* The Ojibwa simply called it *Kitchi-Gami,* or "the great lake." And with his attempt at translating Finnish folk poetry into the American experience, Henry Wadsworth Longfellow called it Big-Sea-Water in *The Song of Hiawatha.* Lake Superior, it seems, needs no fancy label. It's enough to behold the lake and simply say, "Wow, that's a big body of water." And it is. Superior is the largest of the Great Lakes in terms of both acreage and depth.

It wasn't until the 1730s that a sailing ship was seen on Lake Superior. Native peoples traveled by canoe and taught the Europeans to do the same. Often, they paddled the two-person birchbark canoes you imagine, but the voyageurs transported furs in boats 35 feet long. Traveling along the southern shore of Lake Superior presented a particular challenge—a 12-mile stretch of cliffs that offered no safe harbor. It could take several hours to traverse the length of what we now call the Pictured Rocks, plenty of time for an unfortunate change in the weather. As such, the sight of these inspiring sandstone cliffs, with their undulating bands of color, struck in early travelers a sense of urgency if not fear.

"By the shining Big-Sea-Water" lies Twelvemile Beach.

KEY INFORMATION

CONTACT: Pictured Rocks National Lakeshore, 906-387-2607, nps.gov/piro; reservations: 877-444-6777, recreation.gov/camping/campgrounds/247602

OPEN: Year-round but unmaintained in winter

SITES: 36 (2 are wheelchair accessible)

EACH SITE HAS: Picnic table, fire pit, and tent pad

ASSIGNMENT: Online or by phone

REGISTRATION: Self-register at campground

AMENITIES: Potable water (shut off November–April) and vault toilets

PARKING: At sites

NIGHTLY FEE: $20 May–October, $15 November–April

ELEVATION: 639'

RESTRICTIONS

PETS: On leash only

FIRES: Fire pits only

ALCOHOL: No stated restrictions; check ahead to confirm

VEHICLES: 2/site

OTHER: 8 people/site; 14-day stay limit; quiet hours 8 p.m.–8 a.m.; store all food and scented items in bear-proof containers; pack out all trash

Pictured Rocks National Lakeshore encompasses 42 miles of the Lake Superior shoreline, including these famed cliffs. Inland, it includes 11,740 acres of woods, waterfalls, and lakes. This national park has three campgrounds: Hurricane River, Twelvemile Beach, and Beaver Lake. Hurricane River has 21 sites on two loops. Close to Lake Superior, it is also close to Grand Marais (just 12 miles) and has trail access to the Au Sable Light Station. As such, it sees a fair amount of traffic. Near the middle of the park, eight secluded sites on a small inland lake comprise the Beaver Lake Campground. But if you're going to hoof it all the way to the Pictured Rocks, a view of Lake Superior should not be missed, which is why I suggest the 36 sites of the Twelvemile Beach Campground.

The road into the campground passes through a sprawling white-birch forest, carpeted everywhere with ferns. Once the road reaches the lake, it forks to the left and right. To the right, a small parking area gives visitors a chance to stretch their legs and perhaps walk down to the beach or hike a little of the North Country Trail. To the left, campsites are situated down the length of the dirt drive, which has a small oblong loop at the end. High on a bluff, more than half the sites overlook Lake Superior and the beach for which the campground is named. Birches and the occasional pine provide shade.

Amenities at the park's campgrounds are limited to vault toilets and drinkable water. The campground remains open year-round, but during the off-season (November–April) the water is shut off, and in the winter roads are often closed because of snow.

Below the campground, along the lake, Twelvemile Beach stretches from the Pictured Rocks in the west to the Grand Sable Banks near Grand Marais in the east. This beach is just one of several features worth exploring in the park—the Grand Sable Banks and Dunes, Chapel Rock and Beach, Miners Beach and Miners River, and, for a different perspective on the Pictured Rocks themselves, Miners Castle. There are also several waterfalls to discover. Stop by one of the park's visitor centers for a map and information on trails.

Ironically, staying in the park isn't the best way to see the cliffs themselves. For you to really get an idea of what all the fuss is about, the Pictured Rocks should be seen from the water. One option is to bring or rent sea kayaks and paddle out on your own. This is recommended only for skilled paddlers: the waters of Lake Superior can reach into the high 60s in the warmest years, but these are extreme highs—the mid-50s are average for summer. And as I mentioned before, the cliffs offer no sanctuary if the water should turn rough.

The easiest way to get a peek is to take one of the 3-hour boat tours out of Munising offered by **Pictured Rocks Cruises** (906-387-3386, picturedrocks.com). Many travelers will begin and end their experience of the park with one of these afternoon trips. Tours leave fairly regularly in the summer from the City Dock, and the narration includes information on various formations and some history of the Pictured Rocks and nearby Grand Island.

While you're on the Munising side of the park, visit the Munising Falls Interpretive Center. From here, an 800-foot path leads to Munising Falls. Continuing deeper into the park along East Munising Avenue, turn onto Pictured Rock Trails (also called Miners Castle Road and H-11), and follow the signs to the Miners Falls. From the trailhead to the waterfall is just a 0.5-mile hike. Then keep heading north to Miners Castle, which has a picnic area and an overlook of Lake Superior and a section of the Pictured Rocks.

Pictured Rocks National Lakeshore: Twelvemile Beach Campground

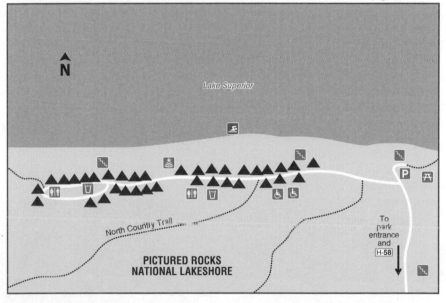

GETTING THERE

The campgrounds at Pictured Rocks National Lakeshore are approached from the Grand Marais side of the park. From the Mackinac Bridge, take I-75 North to Exit 352, and drive north on M-123 about 22 miles; then turn left onto M-28, and continue west 46 miles. At the junction with M-77, turn right (north) and drive 24 miles. In downtown Grand Marais, turn left (west) onto Carlson Street/H-58, and follow the signs 2.7 miles to the Grand Sable Visitor Center. The campground is 12.9 miles farther on H-58, but stopping at the visitor center first is recommended to help you get your bearings.

GPS COORDINATES: N46° 38.646' W86° 12.318'

46

⛺ Porcupine Mountains Wilderness State Park: PRESQUE ISLE CAMPGROUND

Beauty ★★★★★ Privacy ★★★★ Spaciousness ★★★★★ Quiet ★★★★ Security ★★★★★ Cleanliness ★★★★★

The wilderness area preserves the largest virgin stand of northern hardwoods west of the Adirondacks.

From a distance, these humped mountains along the southern shore of Lake Superior, bristling with old-growth northern hardwoods, are said to resemble a crouching porcupine. Henry Schoolcraft, a prodigious 19th-century explorer of the Northwest Territory, recorded the Chippewa name for the range as *Kaug Wudju,* their name for the prickly animal. Today, most people just call them the Porkies. As part of the 59,000-acre Porcupine Mountains Wilderness State Park, the mountains are the backdrop to some of the state's most stunning country. Rising up from the Great Lake to well over a thousand feet, the mountains are lined with hard-worn hiking trails, veined with rivers and streams, and dotted with lakes—including the picturesque Lake of the Clouds.

The wilderness area preserves the largest virgin stand of northern hardwoods west of the Adirondacks. The character this lends to the Porkies is something you can't find elsewhere, and it attracts people from all over who have a lot of options when it comes to deciding how to take in the mountains. For many folks, the Porkies are a day trip. They drive up to the Lake of the Clouds overlook, take a few photos, and continue on their way. Others

Presque Isle Campground, awash in fall color

Photo: Dylan Lee

KEY INFORMATION

CONTACT: Michigan DNR–Porcupine Mountains Wilderness State Park, 906-885-5275, michigan.gov/porkies; reservations: 800-447-2757, midnrreservations.com

OPEN: Mid-May–Mid-October

SITES: 50

EACH SITE HAS: Picnic table and fire pit

ASSIGNMENT: Online or by phone

REGISTRATION: At campground office

AMENITIES: Water and vault toilets

PARKING: At sites

NIGHTLY FEE: $17

ELEVATION: 695'

RESTRICTIONS

PETS: On leash only

FIRES: Fire pits only

ALCOHOL: No stated restrictions; check ahead to confirm

VEHICLES: Michigan Recreation Passport required (see page 8); 2 vehicles/site

OTHER: 6 people/site; 15-day stay limit

---

bring an RV or trailer and set up at the park's modern campground on Union Bay. Near the east entrance, Union Bay is the most popular spot to camp in the Porcupine Mountains. Still others strap on a backpack and head into the backcountry—whether they rent a remote cabin or yurt, or pitch a tent at one of the numerous backpack campsites along the trails, they see more than most visitors of this expansive wilderness.

At the western edge of the park, close to the waterfalls of Presque Isle River, the state park maintains a large, rustic campground. Presque Isle Campground features 50 spacious sites on a lightly wooded bluff overlooking Lake Superior. Generators are allowed only at sites 28–42. That leaves 35 places to pitch your tent with a reasonable assurance of a quiet night. Along the generator side, against the east end of the loop, you'll find a couple of nice sites. Both 34 and 36 are set back among the towering hemlocks, white pines, and maples.

Sites along the northern edge of the campground look down from some height over Lake Superior, but they pay for this view with a lack of privacy from neighboring campers. The choicest spots are at the western end of the main campground. Tent campers can access six walk-in sites by way of a narrow trail into the woods.

The amenities at Presque Isle are spare: vault toilets and water from a hand pump. There is, however, much to recommend the campground over Union Bay or the two smaller rustic sites located along South Boundary Road. From my perspective, the river makes all the difference. As the Presque Isle River finishes out its journey to Lake Superior, it puts on a final show, dropping 100 feet over its last mile. This results in three or four stunning waterfalls.

From the picnic area at the campground, you can cross the river near its mouth over a swinging bridge. Upstream from the bridge, you can see an unnamed falls. A boardwalk leads from the picnic area south along the west side of the river. Hike up the trail for views of Manabezho Falls, Manido Falls, and Nawadaha Falls (a side trail here leads down to the river for a better look). Once you get to South Boundary Road, cross the bridge and make the return trip on the east side of the river.

As you watch gallons of water pound their way down to Lake Superior, it might surprise you that there are people who paddle this river. Only very experienced whitewater kayakers and canoeists will take on the challenge of the lower portions of the Presque Isle River, and even they will portage around many of the falls and rapids, including a stretch of whitewater where the river drops a stunning 140 feet in a mile.

There are a few things not to miss when visiting the Porkies. The Presque Isle waterfalls are just one. The other might just be the most photographed landscape in the state (maybe Michigan's answer to Colorado's Maroon Bells?). That would be the Lake of the Clouds. Located at some elevation behind the first big ridge along Lake Superior, the Lake of the Clouds is stunningly beautiful. Most visitors drive up to the overlook and take in the scenery from the park's viewing platforms. During our last visit, a ranger kindly loaned us her binoculars and pointed out an eagle's nest in the valley below. If that peak doesn't satisfy, consider a hike on the Escarpment Trail.

The Porkies offer miles of hiking paths. The North Country Trail winds through the park, piggybacking on the system established by hikers long ago. The trails from the Presque Isle Campground lead you south along the river for a tour of the waterfalls. Others climb Summit Peak, the highest point in the park. One of the most stunning hikes in the Porcupine Mountains, perhaps in the state, follows the Escarpment Trail and offers breathtaking views of the Lake of the Clouds. The path can turn into a pretty strenuous 8-mile out-and-back, so be sure to know your limitations and check out a park map for ways to cut the trip short.

The Wilderness Visitor Center has maps and information on the park, including its various recreational opportunities.

Porcupine Mountains Wilderness State Park: Presque Isle Campground

GETTING THERE

From M-28 just northeast of Wakefield, turn north onto Presque Isle Road/County Road 519, and continue 16.5 miles to the campground, on your left just before the road dead-ends.

GPS COORDINATES: N46° 42.366' W89° 58.716'

47

Portage Bay State Forest Campground

Beauty ★★★★ Privacy ★★★★★ Spaciousness ★★★★★ Quiet ★★★★★ Security ★★★★★ Cleanliness ★★★★

The sandy lots are tucked behind a long, narrow foredune overgrown with cedar trees, juniper bushes, and ferns.

In all likelihood, Portage Bay got its name from early travelers who used the bay as the beginning of a shortcut across the narrowest point on the Garden Peninsula. Hiking about a mile inland from the water, groups making their way by canoe could pick up Garden Creek, which would lead them out to Garden Bay. The minor inconvenience of this short portage could save them 30 miles of open-water paddling. Many of the bays and harbors on the Great Lakes, especially those along the Upper Peninsula, bear names given them by the French. To the east is Scul Choix Point (pronounced here "sis-shwah"), which once provided a safe place for French trappers caught in a storm. They wryly called it *seul choix,* or "only choice."

I find it fascinating to walk the beach at Portage Bay State Forest Campground and contemplate what kind of men they were who found it easier to lug a canoe (which might carry a dozen men) and hundreds of pounds of furs across the Garden Peninsula than to paddle around it. The campground gives no hint of such arduous choices. At the end of a winding, narrow dirt road, far from US 2 and the civilization it offers, Portage Bay seems a world away, from both its past and our present.

Views of Lake Michigan are often obscured by the trees surrounding this quiet campground.

KEY INFORMATION

CONTACT: Michigan DNR–Fayette Historic State Park, 906-644-2603, tinyurl.com /portagebaycampground

OPEN: Year-round, though snow will prevent road access in winter

SITES: 23

EACH SITE HAS: Picnic table and fire pit

ASSIGNMENT: First come, first served; no reservations

REGISTRATION: Self-register on-site

AMENITIES: Hand-pumped potable water and pit toilets

PARKING: At sites

NIGHTLY FEE: $15

ELEVATION: 586'

RESTRICTIONS

PETS: On leash only

FIRES: Fire pits only

ALCOHOL: No stated restrictions; check ahead to confirm

VEHICLES: Michigan Recreation Passport required (see page 8); 2 vehicles/site

OTHER: 6 people/site; 15-day stay limit

Portage Bay offers 23 sites along a remote stretch of northern Lake Michigan. The sandy lots are tucked away behind a long, narrow foredune that is grown over with cedar trees, juniper bushes, ferns, and the occasional birch. The dune is not so tall; at some sites you can catch the glimmer of sunlight off the water through the trees. Other sites, such as 14, seem to wedge themselves into the sand, creating a sort of natural shelter—perfect for creating a campsite at one with the surrounding terrain.

Surrounded by a cedar forest, the sites are shady, large enough to spread out, and spaced so that you tend to forget the neighbors altogether. At each end, sites 2–4 and 22 and 23, the sandy rise goes to ground and campers enjoy a less obstructed view of the distant lake. These are the ones to pick if you like that morning sunrise coming up over the water.

With the exception of 7, the only site to fall on the west side of the road, trails lead from the individual campsites out to the water. The bay warms up nicely in the summer and is great for swimming.

At the north end of the campground, you will find the trailhead for the Ninga Aki Pathway. This 2.5-mile walk in the woods features 15 interpretive stations describing different natural features and the role they played in the lives of the Ojibwa people. The first of the pathway's two loops takes you back to Bog Lake—portions of the trail follow a boardwalk over wetland. The other loop follows the shore of Lake Michigan before curving back to the campground.

From its base just west of Manistique, the Garden Peninsula stretches south into Lake Michigan. On a regional map, it looks as if it's reaching out to touch the tip of Wisconsin's Door Peninsula. To the west, the peninsula defines Big Bay de Noc, the little sister to Green Bay. The peninsula is, in fact, part of the grand Niagara Escarpment, which stretches from upstate New York to Wisconsin.

On the opposite side of the peninsula, west and a little south, you will find one of the state's most interesting parks—Fayette Historic State Park. The campground at Fayette is comfortable enough. RVs and trailers have room to spare, but the site isn't overdeveloped. Described as semimodern, the campground has vault toilets, hand-pumped water, and electrical service.

Most visitors come to the park to roam through the Fayette Historic Townsite. In the late 1880s, this collection of old buildings was once a bustling company town. The Jackson Iron

Company took iron ore and turned it into pig iron to be shipped to plants making steel. The town sits along a natural harbor, partly hemmed in by a long dolomite cliff. The old furnace complex overlooks the water. Visitors tend to be surprised by how much of the old town is actually left. You can still visit the Shelton Hotel, the old town hall, the machine shop, and the company office. Out on the wooded point that outlines the other side of the harbor, homes of the doctor and company superintendent remain for you to visit. Throughout the summer, boats pull into Snail Shell Harbor and tie up at the dock.

Portage Bay State Forest Campground

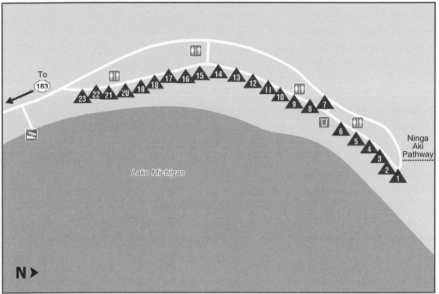

GETTING THERE

From Maple Street in Manistique, follow US 2 west 16 miles to M-183. Turn left (south) and drive 20 miles, passing through the village of Garden along the way. Where M-183 makes a 90-degree turn right (this is the second such turn; the first is just south of Garden), turn left (south) onto LL Road. In 1.3 miles, turn left onto 12.75 Lane—you should see signs—and drive 5 more winding miles generally east. The campground will be on your right just before the road dead-ends.

GPS COORDINATES: N45° 43.434' W86° 32.106'

48

Pretty Lake State Forest Campground

Beauty ★★★★ Privacy ★★★★★ Spaciousness ★★★★ Quiet ★★★★★ Security ★★★★★ Cleanliness ★★★★

Five lakes, each connected by stream or portage trail, are the main features of this quiet area.

North of Newberry, from Whitefish Point across to Grand Marais and the beginning of the Pictured Rocks National Lakeshore, the state maintains a number of small campgrounds within Lake Superior State Forest. Recreational planners here have always had the wisdom to develop campgrounds near lakes and rivers. From Culhane Lake and Bodi Lake northwest of Tahquamenon to the fabled Two-Hearted River and a series of small forest lakes that stretch west almost to Munising, dozens of places to camp can be found.

While all of these campgrounds offer remote locations on scenic lakes and rivers, some are not as well maintained as others. With great trepidation I visited an outhouse on Bodi Lake, the floor of which sank more than 2 inches when I stepped inside. And while I enjoy having a good story to tell, the unfortunate chain of events I was imagining seemed like the kind of story I would rather hear from somebody else. One campground I can recommend without hesitation, however, is the Pretty Lake State Forest Campground, which is part of the greater Pretty Lake Quiet Area.

Five lakes, each connected by stream or portage trail, are the main features of the quiet area. Pretty Lake acts as a portal into this unique preserve—it's the only lake that can be accessed by car. And from here, because motorized boats are prohibited on all the lakes, the

Heavy undergrowth blankets the forest, giving this campground a sense of remote serenity.

KEY INFORMATION

CONTACT: Michigan DNR–Muskallonge Lake State Park, 906-658-3338, tinyurl.com /prettylakecampground

OPEN: Year-round, though snow will prevent road access in winter

SITES: 18

EACH SITE HAS: Picnic table and fire pit

ASSIGNMENT: First come, first served; no reservations

REGISTRATION: Self-register at campground

AMENITIES: Hand-pumped potable water and vault toilets

PARKING: At sites (or parking lot for walk-in sites)

NIGHTLY FEE: $15

ELEVATION: 760'

RESTRICTIONS

PETS: On leash only

FIRES: Fire pits only

ALCOHOL: No stated restrictions; check ahead to confirm

VEHICLES: Michigan Recreation Passport required (see page 8); 2 vehicles/site

OTHER: 6 people/site; 15-day stay limit

only way to explore the area is under your own power. The main campground lies on the northern edge of the lake.

The campground has 18 sites arranged around three loops, about half a dozen of which sit on the water. Facing south toward the lake, these sites allow you to take full advantage of the sun, which can sit pretty low, even in the early and late summer, in these latitudes. Each site is equipped with a wooden picnic table and a fire pit. The vault toilets are on the old side but well maintained.

Beyond these 18, the campground has an additional 5 walk-in sites that offer campers a mini backpacking or wilderness-canoeing adventure. Purely rustic by design, these remote campsites can be found west of Pretty Lake on Camp Eight Lake and Beaverhouse Lake. A trail less than a mile long leads hikers from the parking area near the Pretty Lake boat launch to the sites. Or paddlers can load up their gear in a canoe and get to the sites by water. In keeping with a true canoe-camping experience, the area's lakes are connected with portages (the longest: a 250-foot hike between Camp Eight and Beaverhouse).

Anglers can spend days exploring these lakes. Deep, crystal-clear waters are bordered by a forest of white pines and mixed hardwoods. Deadfall trees along the shore create the perfect habitat for bass. Pretty Lake is on the smallish side. Its 47 acres go deep, however—well over 60 feet deep on the western half of the lake. An able angler should find splake, walleye, and yellow perch. (If you haven't heard of splake, it is the offspring of a male brook trout, also called a speckled trout, and a female lake trout.)

At its deepest, Camp Eight Lake is more than 70 feet. Folks catch rainbow trout, yellow perch, and smallmouth bass. Beaverhouse Lake, also more than 60 feet deep, is known for largemouth bass, walleye, sunfish, and yellow perch.

If your interest leans more toward fly-fishing, you might want to ditch the lakes altogether. Camping at Pretty Lake puts you in easy reach of one of the Upper Peninsula's more famous rivers. Of Ernest Hemingway's short stories, best known perhaps are those that feature his protagonist Nick Adams, who is often a thinly veiled characterization of the author himself. The two-part story that finishes the collection *In Our Time* is titled "Big Two-Hearted River." Hemingway knew the rivers of northern Michigan and found a bit of poetry in the name. In all likelihood, the actual river described in the story is the Fox River, 20 miles or so to the west, but the poetry of the Two-Hearted continues to captivate.

Close to Pretty Lake, three state forest campgrounds—High Bridge, Reed and Green Bridge, and Mouth of the Two-Hearted River—sit alongside this fabled water. Six miles northeast of High Bridge, paddlers can still find the Two-Hearted River Canoe Campground. Though no longer maintained, it's still within the state forest, where wilderness-camping rules apply. In addition to the campgrounds on the river, the state forest maintains another half dozen within a short drive. All would be OK alternatives to Pretty Lake, if you want to stay close to the river for early-morning casts.

Hikers looking to stretch their legs will find that the North Country Trail passes just 5 miles north of the Pretty Lake State Forest Campground. If more noise and speed are what you need, the Pine Ridge Trail and the Two-Hearted Trail for off-road vehicles lie to the north and northeast, respectively. For families looking for more beach, Muskallonge State Park, 8 miles north, straddles the shore of Lake Superior and Muskallonge Lake. While the Great Lake is often too cold for swimming, Muskallonge has a decent swimming beach beside warmer water.

Pretty Lake State Forest Campground

GETTING THERE

From MI-123 in Fourmile Corner, turn left (west) onto County Road 407/H-37, and drive 17.5 miles (after the first 4 miles, the road turns north). Then turn left (west again) onto Forest Service Road 416 (also called Holland Lake Road and Stellwagon Road on maps). In 2.7 miles, turn right (south) onto Pretty Lake Road and, about 0.8 mile farther, look for the campground on the left (southeast) side of the road.

GPS COORDINATES: N46° 36.237' W85° 39.483'

49

⚕ Sylvania Wilderness and Recreation Area: CLARK LAKE CAMPGROUND

Beauty ★★★★★ Privacy ★★★★ Spaciousness ★★★★★ Quiet ★★★★ Security ★★★★★ Cleanliness ★★★★★

Clark Lake is just the beginning when it comes to camping in the Sylvania Wilderness.

Ottawa National Forest manages nearly 1 million acres in Michigan's western Upper Peninsula, and perhaps none of it is as ruggedly beautiful as the 18,327 acres set aside as the Sylvania Wilderness and Recreation Area. In the late 1800s, a lumberman from Wisconsin purchased 80 acres south of Clark Lake, which is several miles southwest of Watersmeet. He was so impressed with the magnificence of the region that he decided to keep the property as a private preserve. He soon introduced others to this primeval forest, and they too snatched up acreage. They soon established the Sylvan Club and built lodges and cabins to better enjoy their rustic playground. In 1967, the U.S. Forest Service purchased the land; 20 years later, the land joined several other tracts recognized by the Michigan Wilderness Act.

Most of the forest in the Upper Peninsula, and the Lower Peninsula for that matter, was harvested in the late 19th and early 20th centuries. What you see today, even in the most remote national and state forests, is second growth, woods less than 100 years old. A few pockets of virgin stands here and there offer a glimpse of the old Michigan. The Sylvania Wilderness offers more than a glimpse. Here you can immerse yourself for a week of camping in an authentic North Country woods.

Autumnal splendor enrobes Clark Lake.

Photo: Peter C. Gorman

KEY INFORMATION

CONTACT: Ottawa National Forest, Waters-meet Ranger District; 906-358-4551, tinyurl.com/sylvaniawildernesscamping; reservations: 877-444-6777, recreation.gov

OPEN: Late May–September

SITES: 48

EACH SITE HAS: Electricity (some sites), picnic table, fire pit with grill, and lantern post

ASSIGNMENT: Online or by phone

REGISTRATION: Self-register at campground, and pay entry fee at the Sylvania Entrance Station

AMENITIES: Pressurized drinking water, flush and vault toilets, and modern restrooms

PARKING: At sites

NIGHTLY FEE: $18 nonelectric, $23 electric, plus $5 day-use fee (annual passes $30) and free wilderness permit (available at trailhead kiosks and the Sylvania Entrance Station)

ELEVATION: 885'

RESTRICTIONS

PETS: On leash only

FIRES: Fire pits only

ALCOHOL: No stated restrictions; check ahead to confirm

VEHICLES: 2/site

OTHER: 8 people site; 14-day stay limit

Not everyone has the resources and opportunity for backcountry adventure, so the Forest Service maintains a regular semimodern campground near the entrance to the wilderness area. The Lake Campground allows campers a chance to spend a few days walking or paddling into the Sylvania Tract without all the gear and preparation that comes with loading up a canoe for a week on the water.

The campground holds 48 sites on four loops. This is a national forest, after all, so it's no surprise to find the campground nestled in the woods, mostly pines interspersed with hardwoods. Campsite spurs are packed gravel, but the sites tend to be grassy. Throughout the camp you will find a nice mix—wooded lots with lots of privacy versus wide-open sites, spaces with room to spread out but also a few cozy nooks tucked into the trees.

The sites here feature the usual national forest campground amenities—wooden picnic table, lantern post, and fire pit with an iron grill. Brick bathrooms with running hot water and flush toilets are spaced evenly throughout, and down by the day-use area you will find men's and women's shower rooms. I can't speak for the ladies, but the men's side is an open locker-room style shower. With its concrete-slab floors and cinderblock walls, this building has seen better days, but if you wait long enough, the water eventually warms a little, and that's enough of a luxury sometimes to overcome dingy surroundings.

Spend much time looking at a map of the Sylvania Tract, as some folks call it, and you will see that Clark Lake is just the beginning when it comes to camping in the Sylvania Wilderness. Another 50 sites are located throughout the park. Most are accessible only by canoe, though there is a nice trail system that passes a number of the sites, and backpackers will use these from time to time.

Paddlers access the wilderness from one of two boat landings. Clark Lake has a parking area, with shower and restroom facilities and a boat launch. The lake has 11 backcountry sites along its shore, and this is the most popular put-in for paddlers heading into the park. The other landing can be found east of the campground along County Road 535. Crooked Lake also has a parking area, and the short trail leading from the parking lot to the boat launch is itself a scenic preview to what awaits visitors making their way into the wild. The waters here are relatively clear. You'll find that many of the Upper Peninsula's lakes and rivers are stained brown by tannins (this is how the Black River and the Tahquamenon's Root Beer Falls get their names). The waters of Sylvania, on the other hand, are a clear blue-green.

The SWRA has often been called Michigan's answer to the Boundary Waters Canoe Area. While not nearly as expansive, with somewhat different geology (Boundary Waters tends to have rockier terrain), Sylvania does offer some of the same North Country charms you find in Minnesota. When planning a trip through the SWRA, campers have fewer options in regards to routes and distances, but once the packs are loaded—whether they are backpacks or Duluth packs—and the trip is under way, the sense of solitude is the same. There is still the soft ripple when a paddle touches the water, the sound of loons calling in the distance, and perhaps an eagle flying high above. And there's the same distance from civilization that campers crave.

Sylvania Wilderness and Recreation Area: Clark Lake Campground

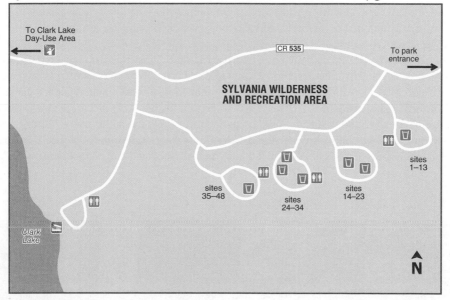

GETTING THERE

Almost exactly 4 miles west of Watersmeet on US 2, turn left (south) onto CR 535/Thousand Island Lake Road. In 4 miles you will come to the Sylvania Entrance Station—turn left (south) and pay the use fee at the entrance booth. Continuing past the entrance booth, the road comes to a T. Turn left (south), and the campground is a couple thousand feet ahead on your left.

GPS COORDINATES: N46° 14.478' W89° 19.248'

50

⛺ Tahquamenon Falls State Park:
RIVERMOUTH PINES CAMPGROUND

Beauty ★★★★★ Privacy ★★★★ Spaciousness ★★★★★ Quiet ★★★★ Security ★★★★★ Cleanliness ★★★★★

The Rivermouth Pines Campground offers the most secluded and picturesque campsites you will find in the park.

Nothing about the upper or lower sections of the Tahquamenon—a quiet river, meandering yet ponderous—hints at the cataclysms in the middle. Springing up from the Tahquamenon Lakes, the river is steeped in tannins as it flows through cedar bogs, giving it a unique copper tone (locals sometimes call it Root Beer Falls). The more dramatic of the two sections, the Upper Falls sends water over a 48-foot drop. At this point the river has expanded to more than 200 feet, creating a wide curtain of falling water. The Lower Falls farther downstream are a combination of five smaller cascades, which are a bit more approachable.

The state park here has three campgrounds: Upper Falls, Lower Falls, and, several miles to the east, Rivermouth. The falls are one of the state's biggest attractions, up there with Mackinac Island, Sleeping Bear Dunes, and Pictured Rocks. Even downstaters who cross the bridge on rare occasions will make a pilgrimage to Tahquamenon at some point, if just for the kids. All of these visitors stop by the Upper Falls parking lot for the short hike to the observation platform. Many stay on to spend money on park concessions, and some even come to camp.

Rivermouth has both a modern and a semimodern campground—choose the latter, called Rivermouth Pines. Off by itself, it offers the most secluded and picturesque campsites

The stillness of the Tahquamenon River belies the beauty of its thundering falls.

KEY INFORMATION

CONTACT: Michigan DNR–Tahquamenon Falls State Park, 906-492-3415, michigan .gov/tahquamenonfalls; reservations: 800-447-2757, midnrreservations.com

OPEN: Late April–early October

SITES: 36

EACH SITE HAS: Picnic table and fire pit

ASSIGNMENT: Online or by phone

REGISTRATION: At campground office

AMENITIES: Water and vault toilets; flush toilets and showers available at neighboring modern campground

PARKING: At sites

NIGHTLY FEE: $17 rustic, $20 semimodern

ELEVATION: 626'

RESTRICTIONS

PETS: On leash only

FIRES: Fire pits only

ALCOHOL: Permitted

VEHICLES: Michigan Recreation Passport required (see page 8); 2 vehicles/site

OTHER: 6 people/site; 15-day stay limit

---

you'll find in the park. The road through the semimodern campground parallels the gentle curve of the Tahquamenon River. For most of its length, the campground has sites on both sides of the road. All are great. Even campers back against the woods have a view of the water. To prevent erosion of the riverbank, the park restricts access to the water to certain areas. Campers with sites on the water will have to carry canoes (and themselves) to one of these points of entry.

Sites 106 and 107 share a small clearing, surrounded by cedars and birches. A clump of trees serves as a boundary between the two sites; otherwise, they enjoy privacy from the rest of the campsites. The sites are on the wooded side of the road but have an unobstructed view of the river. Farther on (sites 120 and above), the woods open; plenty of trees shelter the sites, but there's less undergrowth. Amenities in the semimodern campground include vault toilets and water from a hand-pumped well. A short walk through the woods, however, takes you to Rivermouth's modern campground, with flush toilets and showers.

As it gets closer to Lake Superior, the river bends and winds as if trying to delay the inevitable emptying into the Great Lake. The river mouth itself is across from the campground. A small picnic area, boat launch, and fishing dock give access to the river where it meets Whitefish Bay. This small roadside park seems to be used mostly by fishermen and others looking to put a boat in the water. It's worth a visit—even a short one—to see the contrast between the steel blue of the lake as it is filled with the river's rusty water.

The North Country Trail passes through the Tahquamenon Falls State Park, linking Rivermouth Campground with the Upper and Lower Falls before continuing north toward Lake Superior and the Pictured Rocks National Lakeshore. But this is hardly the only opportunity to experience the wilderness areas of the state park. With more than 46,000 acres of rivers, lakes, and streams, the park has enough trails here for multiday trips into the park, and numerous loops make excellent day hikes. Even exploring the falls can turn into an opportunity for a relaxing walk in the woods—consider the 4-mile River Trail, which connects the Upper and Lower Falls.

The area's other big attraction is the wildlife. Nearby, the town of Newberry touts itself as Michigan's Official Moose Capital, and it's not uncommon for visitors to see deer, black bears, and eagles in the park. The state publishes a moose-viewing guide, *Michigan Moose,* which you can pick up at the visitor center.

Because Tahquamenon Falls State Park enjoys a steady flow of visitors throughout the summer, concessions here are particularly good. In addition to the usual snack station, you'll find the **Tahquamenon Falls Brewery & Pub** (tahquamenonfallsbrewery.com), a full-service sit-down restaurant, near the Upper Falls. With a surprisingly extensive menu and excellent microbrews, it's one of the nicest places to eat in the area.

From the town of Paradise on M-123, it's only 10 miles to Whitefish Point. For a side trip, consider spending the day on the point exploring the **Whitefish Point Light Station** and **Great Lakes Shipwreck Museum** (18335 N. Whitefish Point Road; 906-492-3747, shipwreck museum.com). This complex used to be a Coast Guard station, the light guiding ships around the point and into Whitefish Bay. Many know it today as the eastern end of Lake Superior's "shipwreck coast." The museum does more than just tell the stories of the ships and sailors who fell upon hard times on these lakes—it uses sound and creative lighting to take visitors down through the darkling water, giving the displays of recovered artifacts and models of shipwrecks a haunting context. Most visitors recognize the memorial to the *Edmund Fitzgerald.* In 1975, a mere 17 miles from Whitefish Bay, the freighter sank, taking with it the ship's entire crew. The museum displays the ship's 200-pound bronze bell.

Tahquamenon Falls State Park: Rivermouth Pines Campground

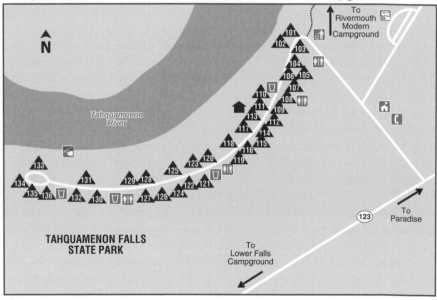

GETTING THERE

From the Mackinac Bridge, take I-75 North to Exit 352, and follow M-123 north and west 50.3 miles. The campground will be on your left before M-123 crosses the Tahquamenon River, about 5 miles south of the village of Paradise.

GPS COORDINATES: N46° 33.366' W85° 02.124'

APPENDIX A

CAMPING EQUIPMENT CHECKLIST

Camping is more fun when you can enjoy it at a moment's notice. You never know when the opportunity may arise to head for the woods—and when it does, wouldn't it be nice to be able to pack your car with all the essentials, drawn from prepacked boxes carefully cleaned, resupplied, and stored after your last trip?

COOKING UTENSILS
Aluminum foil
Bottles of salt, pepper, spices, sugar, cooking
    oil, and condiments in waterproof, spillproof
    containers
Bowls
Can opener
Cooking pots with lids
Cooler
Corkscrew
Cups (plastic or tin)
Dish soap (biodegradable), dishcloth, and towel
Dutch oven and fire pan
Fire starter
Flatware
Food of your choice
Frying pan and spatula
Lighter, matches in waterproof container
Paper towels
Plates
Pocketknife
Stove and fuel
Strainer
Tablecloth
Trash bags
Wooden spoon

SLEEPING GEAR
Pillow
Sleeping bag
Sleeping pad (inflatable or insulated)
Tent with ground tarp and rainfly

MISCELLANEOUS
Bath soap (biodegradable), washcloth, and towel
Camp chairs
Candles
Compass
Day pack
Extra batteries (for flashlight and electronics)
First aid kit (see page 6)
Flashlight/headlamp
GPS unit
Lantern
Maps (road, trail, topographic, etc.)
Moist towelettes
Saw/ax
Sunglasses
Toilet paper
Water bottle(s)
Wool blanket
Zip-top plastic bags

APPENDIX B

SOURCES OF INFORMATION

GRAND TRAVERSE COUNTY PARKS & RECREATION
231-922-4818
co.grand-traverse.mi.us/764/parks-recreation

MICHIGAN DEPARTMENT OF NATURAL RESOURCES
michigan.gov/dnr

Au Sable State Forest
Grayling Forest Management Unit
989-348-6371

Copper Country State Forest
Crystal Falls Forest Management Unit
906-875-6622

Escanaba River State Forest
Gwinn Forest Management Unit
906-346-9201

Lake Superior State Forest
Newberry Forest Management Unit
906-293-3293

Mackinaw State Forest
Atlanta Forest Management Unit
989-785-4251

Pere Marquette State Forest
Cadillac Forest Management Unit
231-775-9727

Pigeon River Country State Forest
Pigeon River Forest Management Unit
989-983-4101

Sault Ste. Marie Forest Management Unit
906-635-5281

Shingleton Forest Management Unit
906-452-6227

Traverse City Forest Management Unit
231-922-5280

NATIONAL PARK SERVICE
nps.gov

Pictured Rocks National Lakeshore
906-387-2607, nps.gov/piro

Sleeping Bear Dunes National Lakeshore
231-326-5134, nps.gov/slbe

U.S. FOREST SERVICE
fs.usda.gov

Hiawatha National Forest
906-786-4062, fs.usda.gov/hiawatha

Huron–Manistee National Forest
800-821-6263, fs.usda.gov/hmnf

Ottawa National Forest
906-932-1330, fs.usda.gov/ottawa

INDEX

ABOUT THE AUTHOR

A native Michigander, Matt Forster has camped all around the Great Lakes, the Rockies, New England, and now Texas. He's carried his gear in backpacks, Duluth packs, saddlebags, and car trunks and slept in tents, pop-ups, camper vans, and RVs. He has two children who have discovered the joy of camping through Scouting. These days, camping trips often come down to tossing the tent in the back of the car, loading up way too much equipment, and praying for good weather (a necessity with two kids in tow).

Matt's other books are *Backroads & Byways of Michigan* (The Countryman Press), *Backroads & Byways of Ohio* (The Countryman Press), *Colorado: An Explorer's Guide* (The Countryman Press), *Best Hikes Near Detroit and Ann Arbor* (FalconGuides), and *Best Hikes Near Houston* (FalconGuides).

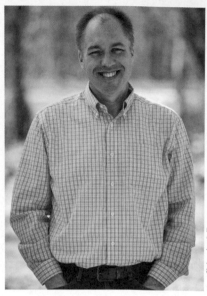

Photo: Christopher Belli